Please return or renew this
item by the last date shown.
You may renew books by phone
0345 60 80 195 or the internet

East Sussex
County Council

**CROWBOROUGH LIBRARY, PINE GROVE,
CROWBOROUGH, TN6 1DH
Tel: 0345 60 80 195**

Library and Information Service
eastsussex.gov.uk/libraries

ROUTLEDGE MODERN AND CONTEMPORARY DRAMATISTS
Series editors: Maggie B. Gale and Mary Luckhurst

Routledge Modern and Contemporary Dramatists is a new series of innovative and exciting critical introductions to the work of internationally pioneering playwrights. The series includes recent *and* well-established playwrights and offers primary materials on contemporary dramatists who are under-represented in secondary criticism. Each volume provides detailed cultural, historical and political material, examines selected plays in production, and theorises the playwright's artistic agenda and working methods, as well as their contribution to the development of playwriting and theatre.

Volumes currently available in the series are:

J.B. Priestley by Maggie B. Gale
Federico García Lorca by Maria M. Delgado
Susan Glaspell and Sophie Treadwell by Barbara Ozieblo and Jerry Dickey

Future volumes will include:

Caryl Churchill by Mary Luckhurst
Mark Ravenhill by John Deeney
Jean Genet by David Bradby
August Strindberg by Eszter Szalczer
Anton Chekhov by Rose Whyman

J.B. Priestley

Routledge Modern and Contemporary Dramatists

Maggie B. Gale

Routledge
Taylor & Francis Group

LONDON AND NEW YORK

First published 2008 by Routledge
2 Park Square, Milton Park, Abingdon, Oxon OX14 4RN

Simultaneously published in the USA and Canada
by Routledge
270 Madison Avenue, New York, NY 10016

*Routledge is an imprint of the Taylor & Francis Group, an informa
business*

© 2008 Maggie B. Gale

Typeset in Sabon and Georgia by
Keystroke, 28 High Street, Tettenhall, Wolverhampton
Printed and bound in Great Britain by
TJ International Ltd, Padstow, Cornwall

British Library Cataloguing in Publication Data
A catalogue record for this book is available from the British Library

Library of Congress Cataloging in Publication Data
Gale, Maggie B. (Maggie Barbara), 1963–
J.B. Priestley/Maggie B. Gale.
        p. cm. — (Routledge modern and contemporary dramatists)
    Includes bibliographical references and index.
    1. Priestley, J. B. (John Boynton), 1894–1984.   I. Title.
    PR6031.R6Z568 2008
    828′.91209—dc22   2007027018

ISBN 10: 0–415–40242–5 (hbk)
ISBN 10: 0–415–40243–3 (pbk)
ISBN 10: 0–203–93262–5 (ebk)

ISBN 13: 978–0–415–40242–2 (hbk)
ISBN 13: 978–0–415–40243–9 (pbk)
ISBN 13: 978–0–203–93262–9 (ebk)

Contents

Illustrations

Acknowledgements

I would like to thank the University of Manchester, the Arts and Humanities Research Council, England, and Michael and Lara Gale, Austin, Texas for financing and supporting this project. Colleagues and friends have patiently provided both comradely and intellectual support, especially Ann Featherstone, Liz A. Gale, John F. Deeney, John Stokes, Maria Delgado, Mary Luckhurst, Rose Whyman, Sue Gilligan, James Thompson, Viv Gardner and Matthew Frost. Thanks also to Talia Rodgers and Minh-Ha Duong at Routledge, to Tom Priestley and to Jim Gill at PFD for permission to publish extensively from Priestley's works. I am grateful to Norma Campbell Vickers and Alena Kyncl for permission to reprint their late husbands' photographs of productions of Priestley plays, and to Keith Pattison and the West Yorkshire Playhouse for the photographs of Patrick Stewart in Jude Kelly's *Johnson Over Jordan* (2001). Research assistants at the Harry Ransom Humanities Research Center in Austin, Texas, the Theatre Museum, London and Richard Mangan at the Raymond Mander and Joe Mitchenson Theatre Collection provided vital materials with great patience. Particular thanks to Alison Cullingford in Special Collections at the University of Bradford Library: her expertise and kindness have been invaluable. All extracts and material from the works of J.B. Priestley are reproduced by permission of PFD (www.pfd.co.uk) on behalf of the Estate of J.B. Priestley. Excerpt from Part I of 'Burnt Norton' in *Four Quartets* by T.S. Eliot, copyright The Estate, reprinted by permission of the publisher. Permission to reprint the same, gratefully acknowledged from Faber and Faber Ltd, England.

This book is dedicated to my beloved and greatly missed father Tony Gale (23 April 1937–22 August 2006), whose J.B. Priestley play volumes I stole as a teenager.

Part I
Life, politics and theory

1   Life, career and politics

Overview

J.B. Priestley (1894–1984) was born into a lower-middle-class family in Bradford, England at the close of the nineteenth century. A playwright, novelist, essayist, broadcaster and socialist-humanist, he left school in his mid-teens, and went into the wool trade as a clerk. It was during this period, before his time on the Front in France during the First World War (1914–18), that he began a writing career which was to span almost a century, one in which much of the vast social and cultural change was reflected in the work he produced.

> His career demonstrated a new thread of mobility in the classes from working and lower middle to middle-class professional which remained an unrealised dream in general but was supremely epitomised in his own life. So many phases in his development were representative of unfolding English history between the years 1894 and 1984.
>
> (Brome 1988: 485)

John Boynton (or 'Jack') Priestley was one of the most prolific and versatile English writers of the twentieth century: he worked across journalism, criticism, literature, theatre, film and radio. He experienced varying levels of success in each medium, and rarely worked solely in any one field at any one time. A socialist at heart and in practice, he believed that the creative arts, both in terms of production and consumption, had a vital importance to society at large and to the individual in particular. Priestley was both a populist and an intellectual, a man of letters and a man of the people, and his plays remain popular and have retained a remarkable cultural currency in the present day. Although much critical reference is made to his written output in general, this volume focuses on Priestley the playwright, theatre theorist and practitioner; he wrote a great deal about theatre, the arts and cultural production, as well as writing over thirty works for the stage. Like Bertolt Brecht, he did not sit quietly in the darkened auditorium while others produced his work, nor did he rely on others to find theatres in which to produce it. Throughout his theatre career, he was a proactive playwright, setting up a production company, keeping a close eye on critical debates and trying to find ways in which he could push the possibilities of playwriting as a creative art into new frontiers and forms. Others have also seen a parallel with Brecht.

> I see him . . . as in one way to be bracketed with Noël Coward. He's prolific, his plays *work*, they generally only have one set and a reasonable size of cast . . . He's practical, he's a man of the theatre. But in another sense he can justly be compared with Brecht, he goes as deep . . . when one realizes what his plays are *really* about, then one perceives that he is just as big as Brecht, that his themes have huge sweep and grandeur.
>
> (Braine 1978: 141)

Although a socialist by conviction, Priestley did not share Brecht's Marxist leanings, but was equally not a 'party' man. He was influenced by developments in scientific and political thinking as well as by Jungian psychology: his processing of these developments filtered through into his plays as well as his theories of theatre, drama and the social function of the arts.

The analysis of Priestley's contribution to British theatre generally and playwriting in particular remains somewhat bound to the received critical and historical framing of British theatre between the two world wars and into the early 1950s. Here, dominant historical narratives focus on subsidised theatres and on 1956 and John Osborne's *Look Back in Anger* as a perceived turning point in the development of drama in Britain. Although challenged by a number of recent theatre histories (see Gale 1996; Luckhurst 2006; Rebellato 1999), such narratives privilege the marginal avant-garde and the non-commercial sections of the industry: such 'longstanding . . . prejudices', which hark back to the nineteenth century binary oppositions of the legitimate and the non-legitimate theatre, mean that other key periods and kinds of work remain unexamined (see Savran 2004). The context in which Priestley worked was that of a *commercial* theatre industry, differing in essence from its European counterparts in its complete lack of government subsidy. J.B. Priestley fought this system, through the ways in which he operated as a playwright and a producer, but it provided the economic background to his theatre career. Some theatre histories of the period (see Chothia 1996; Davies 1987) would have us believe that there was nothing of worth being produced in the commercial West End during the interwar years (1918–39), the period which saw Priestley's debut works in production. Others, however, have pointed to the breadth and depth of plays produced and to the fact that the commercial production system relied on cross-fertilisation from all areas of the 'theatre world' – including the independent, club and subscription theatres (Barker and Gale 2000; Kershaw 2004). Thus, a reappraisal of Priestley's practice in the theatre requires a close examination of the context in which that work took place.

This volume offers a re-evaluation of Priestley's theatre writing from a number of perspectives. Part I provides an overview of the political and ideological beliefs which drove his work, as well as a documentation and analysis of his theories of theatre and drama, his critique of the critics and his vision of the function of theatre as a form of cultural production. For Priestley theatre helped to define culture, in a society which was undergoing radical and swift social and economic transformation. In Part II, his major plays are grouped thematically and are discussed both in terms of their original production and reception and in terms of the ensuing critical analyses by academics and theatre historians. Finally, Part III focuses on a range of productions of three of his works, *The*

Good Companions (1931), *An Inspector Calls* (1946) and *Johnson Over Jordan* (1939). Important materials from major theatre archives, as well as evidence from biographies, autobiographies, interviews and critical works are brought to bear on this re-evaluation of J.B. Priestley, one of the most popular, prolific, and often experimental, British playwrights of the twentieth century.[1]

Life and career: from Bradford to the West End

There are a number of biographies of J.B. Priestley, all of which offer a different focus in terms of their construction of a picture of Priestley's life (Brome 1988; Cook 1997; Cooper 1970). Many of them borrow heavily from Priestley's own autobiographical writing (Priestley 1940, 1941a, 1962, 1977), often without, however, attempting to authenticate or reflect upon the ways in which Priestley wrote about himself. Similarly many of the biographies fail to identify or challenge the various social, political and academic prejudices which have historically underpinned readings of his work. This part of the book uses the broad framework of these collective 'depictions of a life' as a means of charting the interrelationship between his life, career and ideological thinking. The son of a school teacher in the northern industrial community of Bradford, and a student of literature studying on an officer's scholarship at the University of Cambridge immediately after the First World War, his origins influenced the development of his political thinking and in turn filtered into every aspect of his career in theatre.

> after the war I turned away from politics, not because my political sympathies had changed but because I felt I needed a private world of a few friends and a lot of books . . . I became the typical Englishman behind his high wall and closed door . . .
>
> Oddly enough it was not politics but the Theatre that opened the door and broke down the wall for me. In the early Thirties I turned from novels and essays to plays, and it happened that from the first I took more interest in the actual

production of my plays than the average playwright does
. . . I found myself at last leaving the quiet study . . . for the
bustle and confusion and the concerted effort of theatrical
production. . . . There might be more heartbreaks in the
production of a play than in the publication of a book, but
there was also much more fun. And something too that was
more than fun – a sense of kinship with my fellow workers
in the Theatre.

(*Letter to a Returning Serviceman*, Priestley 1945b: 27)

J.B. Priestley's professional work in the theatre began in the early
1930s, and as he suggests in his *Letter to a Returning Serviceman*
(1945), this new career pathway led him to a different, more
collective way of working. Biographers and critics vary as to the
degree to which they investigate Priestley's theatre work: some
focus on his plays more than others (Atkins 1981; Braine 1978;
Evans 1964). There is, however, an overall acknowledgement that
Priestley's theatre work was central to his career from the early
1930s through to the late 1950s. Equally, theatre features in a
great deal of his fictional writing, in novels such as *The Good
Companions* (1929), *Jenny Villiers* (1947) and *Lost Empires*
(1965); later in life he used theatre as a metaphor for modes of
self-reflection and the processing of internal dialogue.

We carry a theatre around with us, and we should enjoy the
comedy inside. What goes on in our inner world can soon be
turned into an enjoyable comedy if we stop hugging and
petting our injured vanity, our jealousy and envy.

(Priestley 1972: 32–3)

Here, late in life, Priestley is referring to the mediation of public
and private selves, a process with which he was familiar and one
that is vital in the biographical works of which he is the subject.
Thus Vincent Brome is rather scathing about a great deal of
Priestley's writing (Brome 1988), but focuses very heavily on
Priestley's private relationships with women; his three wives, his
supposed mistresses, and on his relationships with his children.
Judith Cook, emphasising empirical social and historical research,

gives a more balanced, detailed and contextualised analysis of Priestley's life. She stresses the early influences of his childhood community and his years spent in action in France during the First World War (Cook 1997). Doubtless, these years, from September 1914 where he witnessed the atrocities of the war as a soldier in the trenches, to March 1919, when he left the army, hugely influenced Priestley's writing life. Yet a number of critics have pointed to the fact that Priestley himself wrote relatively little about his war experience (Atkins 1981; Cooper 1970). He did not find in war 'the deeper reality we all look for'; it did not transform him into an artist in the way it did others of his generation (Priestley 1962: 87).

> When I look back on my life . . . these four-and-a-half years shrink at once; they seem nothing more than a queer bend in the road full of dust and confusion. But when memory really goes to work and I re-enter those years, then just because they used up all my earlier twenties . . . they suddenly turn into a whole epoch, almost another life in another world . . . I think the First War cut deeper and played more tricks with time because it was first, because it was bloodier, because it came out of a blue that nobody saw after 1914. The map that came to pieces in 1939 was never the apparently solid arrangement that blew up in 1914.
>
> (Priestley 1962: 86)

For Priestley, dramatic representations of the 1914–18 war, relatively late to arrive on the interwar West End stages (see Barker and Gale 2000), such as R. C. Sherriff's play *Journey's End* (1928), presented trench life as 'dry and commodious' rather like a 'suite in some Grand Hotel' (Priestley 1962: 99–100). Priestley's war finds its way into his writing through a continual return to the pre-1914 period, and through his sustained effort to encourage a process of self reflection in terms of our responsibilities as members of a community both nationally and internationally, rather than in overt and detailed accounts of his own actual war experience. His political views were sharpened and clarified, first by his war experience, and second through his time as a student in the early 1920s at Cambridge, which, much like Oxford, was still the enclave of the upper-middle and ruling classes. Here Priestley, whose promotion to the officer class had brought with it the possibility of a university grant, largely studied among younger men, from a very different class, predominantly from the south of England and educated in the private sector. Again, he does not write much about these years, during which he married, became a father and graduated. Later in life, however, he was very sceptical of certain types of Leavisite academic criticism which he saw as delimiting the boundaries of the purpose and function of literature, something which will be expanded upon later.

Following his degree, he turned down the offer of academic employment and began what was to become a long career as an essayist, journalist and critic. The success of his novel *The Good Companions* in 1929 afforded him financial stability and the possibility of creative experiment. By the early 1930s he began writing for theatre; his first play was an adaptation of *The Good Companions* (1931) written with Edward Knoblock. The second was *Dangerous Corner* (1932), which the celebrated author and critic Rebecca West (see Stokes 1996) thought contained 'real dialogue with proper nerves in the sentences'. West congratulated him for having written so 'rigorous and exciting' a play, one which 'refreshed . . . after the chopped hay of the ordinary English play'.[2] Although seen by some as a relative failure in terms of its original West End production run (Brome 1988; Cook 1997), *Dangerous Corner* became one of Priestley's most performed plays. His next play, *Laburnum Grove* (1933), originally ran for over 300 performances.

During the twenty-two years which cover the interwar period, London productions of plays rarely ran for more than 100 performances. Although occasionally there are years when the figure for productions lasting for 100 performances or more is as high as 46 per cent, the average figure is much lower at between 11 and 30 per cent. Unusually then, twelve of Priestley's plays ran for more than 100 performances, and eight of these for more than 200 during their first West End production runs. There is no consistency in the 'types' of plays which proved most popular; *The Good Companions* (1931), *Laburnum Grove* (1933), *Time and the Conways* (1937), *I Have Been Here Before* (1937), *When We Are Married* (1938), *They Came to a City* (1943), *How Are They at Home?* (1944), *Ever Since Paradise* (1947) and *The Linden Tree* (1947) reveal often radically different approaches to dramatic writing. Priestley succeeded with comedy as much as with 'plays of ideas' and social observation. He consistently found audiences from the 1930s onwards. He would often have more than one play running in the West End at any one time, as well as simultaneous productions in continental Europe or in North America. Equally, his work continues to receive revivals all over the world in both professional and amateur contexts; the most recent and extraordinary example of this was British director Stephen Daldry's National Theatre production of *An Inspector Calls* (1946) in 1992, which transferred from the subsidised sector into the West End, saw numerous international productions and was still touring England in 2005 (see Chapter 7). Very few other English playwrights could match his popularity during his heyday and fewer still have managed to sustain their cultural currency with audiences so consistently.

Life and career: from the West End to the post Second World War years

It is important to stress that Priestley continued with his other writing while working in the theatre. From the 1930s through to the early 1950s he produced more than fifteen novels, critical and autobiographical works. It is inappropriate to talk of Priestley's career in the singular: by contemporary standards he had at least three careers running simultaneously. His autobiographical works all give evidence of an almost workaholic attitude to his professional life. He wrote to a regular schedule, and his life was shaped around his work. By the early 1930s he was well into his second marriage to Jane Wyndham Lewis (née Bannerman) and father to five children, adoptive father to one (Cook 1997). By the 1940s he was also working in radio and film and had gained a public celebrity status which he found somewhat intrusive as his circle of fans grew wider and ever more quick to recognise him in public places.

Figure 1 J.B. Priestley: wartime broadcasting for the BBC.

Priestley's wartime radio broadcasts, known as the Sunday night 'Postscripts', brought his voice into the homes of all classes of British people. For a wartime audience he became a new kind of 'radio personality': the 'first non-politician to whom listeners regularly tuned to hear his personal political and philosophical views' (Nicholas 1995: 248). Begun in early 1940, his broadcasts stopped at his own request and then came back on air during 1941 only to be taken off again by both the BBC and the Ministry of Information, neither of whom would admit responsibility for doing so. Priestley himself suggests that as their political content became more overt, with frequent references to the politics of post-war reconstruction, the broadcasts became too controversial (Priestley 1967a: xix). The public, however, showed great support for his radio work as did other writers; Rebecca West wrote to thank him for them and for Storm Jameson, writer and journalist, they were 'far and away the best'; she also suggested that in them he found 'the poetry of the English'.[3] For others, Priestley's wartime radio broadcasts – the 'Postscripts' and those for the BBC Overseas Service – had an ambassadorial quality: the high-profile politician Ernest Bevin suggested 'you have put over, in your own most effective and individual way, what we are trying to do here and, for this, the whole country owes you a debt of gratitude'.[4] Those with political leanings to the right did not appreciate the growing level of dissent in Priestley's broadcasts, but for many, in a war-torn England which relied on the radio for news and to some extent for comfort, they represented the 'voice of the people'. Some even suggest that he 'brought the BBC's established traditions of impartiality and anonymity into conflict with its new needs: personality and mass appeal' (Nicholas 1995: 266).

Life: a man through the eyes of others

Priestley had homes in London, on the Isle of Wight and later in Stratford-upon-Avon; from each he worked, entertained and travelled. His homes were often full of guests – writers, theatre people and other friends. Priestley worked and socialised with many of the key figures from all aspects of the British arts scene from the 1920s onwards, although few of these were from the so-called elitist sections of the 'highbrow' literary world, a point that is taken up later in this chapter. There were the actors and producers who worked on the many productions of his plays, including Basil Dean, Ralph Richardson, Peggy Ashcroft, Michael Macowan, Irene Hentschel and John Gielgud, publishers and critics such as Rupert Hart-Davis (see Hart-Davis 1991), and other playwrights and writers like George Bernard Shaw and J.M. Barrie. He also kept up a sustained correspondence with prominent critics (see Agate 1946, 1948, 1949) and publicly engaged in critical debates about literature, the arts and social issues both in the national press and in more selective periodicals such as the *Spectator* and the *New Statesman*. Priestley actively engaged with public and political debate more than any playwright of his day.

A wide range of those who worked in theatre and the arts during the first half of the twentieth century mention Priestley in their autobiographies: their depictions of his character, on both a professional and personal level, vary enormously. Theatre historians have warned of the dangers of reading autobiography as somehow an 'authentic' account (Postlewait 2000), although increasingly others suggest that autobiography can be read as an expression of experience and throw light on the relationship between the private and public lives of those working in the theatre industries (Bratton 2003; Gale and Gardner 2004). Priestley's own autobiographies are often structured as travelogues or thought-diaries; he interweaves details of the phases of his career with commentaries on how he viewed these phases and the influence of other contemporary thinkers on his work. The autobiographies are reflective and often self-critical; he rarely mentions his dealings with other 'celebrities' or tries to construct his 'autobiographical self' around the status of others – a strategy common in the autobiographies and biographies of many theatre people (see Bratton 2003).

The actor Alec Guinness remembers lunches and discussions about theatre with Priestley at the Ivy Restaurant, London (Guinness 1997: 54), one of the haunts of the celebrity elite, while Charlie Chaplin counted him among the friends he would always try to visit when in London (Chaplin 1964: 516). The fact of his class origins and his physical largeness often feature in autobiographical portrayals, and the image of 'Jolly Jack Priestley' is frequently located as a counterpoint to his strong political beliefs, his allegedly gruff manner and his obsession with work. Biographers, as already indicated, might stress the frequency of his extra-marital affairs; thus Brome (1988) insists that he hounded the actress Peggy Ashcroft while others present the affair as being more mutual (Cook 1997; O'Connor 1988). For O'Connor, Priestley was at the height of his 'fame and power' in the early 1930s: 'Forceful and strong, his heavy build made him appear solid and reassuring to women' (O'Connor 1998: 25). Yet he also suggests that Ashcroft found herself put off by Priestley's 'potato face, his gruff manner and brooding personality' (O'Connor 1998: 27). Whatever the appeal, her affairs with other theatre practitioners of the era – Theodore Komisarjevsky and Michel St Denis – suggest that she was attracted by Priestley's politics and his search for an innovative theatre which offered more than superficial entertainment.

Depictions of Priestley's personality by those who knew him also vary and range from popular author of fiction and chronicler of English life and humour, to loud proclaimer of socialism or arrogant man of letters and social critic. Alec Guinness's memory of a reported conversation with Ralph Richardson, one of Priestley's favourite actors, who performed in a number of his plays, attests to a certain snobbery about Priestley's wealth and class origins. Richardson remembers being cut out of Priestley's circle for a short while after commenting that his 'brand new and flashy car' was vulgar (Guinness 1986: 271). The impression given by Guinness, notably after Priestley's death, is one of a rather controlling and egocentric man with more money than sense, and an aesthetic taste which hinted at his class origins in its effect of displaying his wealth. Such depictions reveal English social prejudice about the status of earned as opposed to inherited wealth. Certainly, Priestley had to scrape a living until the early 1930s; he had no private income and was financially responsible for a young family. Others, like the writer Ted Willis, remember Priestley's extraordinary generosity: he once offered Willis enough money to support himself for a year so that he could write in relative economic freedom (Willis 1991: 13–14).

In contrast to the media construction of 'Jolly Jack', Priestley often contributed to the depiction of himself as surly and arrogant. One construction of a reported conversation between Priestley and Binkie Beaumont, the premier West End producer from the 1930s and 1940s, shows Priestley as gruff and dismissive. His response to Beaumont – of whose taste and management style Priestley openly disapproved – when asked if he would write a star 'vehicle' for one of Beaumont's contracted actors was, 'I've no time for bloody stars or the star system. If I had my own way, we wouldn't have them. Just a lot of good actors'. According to Beaumont's biographer they never communicated again (Huggett 1989: 540). Yet it was Tennant Plays, the educational branch of Beaumont's company, H.M. Tennant Ltd, which produced the long running *They Came to a City* in 1943 (Duff 1995: 54). Priestley had reported the conversation to Huggett in the 1980s, verifying the myth of hostility between the two men and the different aspects of the theatre scene which they represented, while Huggett wanted to pitch Beaumont as an entrepreneur who had to work against the odds.

Priestley's later autobiographical writing reveals a man deep in thought about his professional achievements (see Priestley 1972, 1977). But just as in reality the lines between the terrains of his professional life were blurred, so too he found affirmation from artists with very different political and professional profiles. Many of those who worked with him in theatre found his intensity and seriousness daunting, and this is often reflected in the ways in which they 'narrativise' their experiences of him. But the numerous Priestley archives, which include letters from Noël Coward, Somerset Maugham, Terence Rattigan and T.S. Eliot, among others traditionally seen as being from the political right, present a somewhat different picture. Aspects of Priestley's work and his personality were admired from all corners of the ideological boxing ring. The complexities of these relationships say more about the nature of the auto/biographical industry and the varying constructions of theatre history, than they do about Priestley's personality, one which was at the same time extrovert and yet deeply introverted. This point is perhaps best illustrated through his correspondence with the psychologist Carl Jung, whose ideas greatly influenced Priestley from the 1930s onwards. For Jung, Priestley's was a 'friendly human voice among the stupid and malevolent noises issuing from the scribbler infested jungle', and having read a number of his plays and novels he noted:

> I was particularly impressed by the two aspects of your personality. Your one face is so much turned to the world that one is surprised, again and again to meet another face which is turned to the great abyss of all things . . . I appreciate the superhuman faculty of looking at things with a straight and with an inverted eye.[5]

Jung's analysis of Priestley, who had visited him on a number of occasions as well as circulating his theories to a British public more familiar with Freudian ideas (Rose 1985), describes a man who was able to be on the outside looking in, at the same time as being in the middle of, and often the cause of, events. This is as true of the various personal depictions of Priestley, as it is of an overview of his work. He did not suffer fools gladly but was always prepared to support and promote the social 'underdog'.

Priestley's success and popularity in the 1920s and 1930s afforded him a prominent social position and his lecture tours, broadcasts and journalism as well as his literary work, brought him into contact with political figures and campaigns throughout the interwar years and well into the 1960s. By the 1960s, now married to Jacquetta Hawkes, an anthropologist with whom he had shared political campaigning and co-written, among other works, the experimental play *Dragon's Mouth* (Hawkes and Priestley 1952), Priestley's energies were spent writing accessible social and literary histories and critical essays such as *The Edwardians* (1970), *English Humour* (1976) and the extra-ordinarily accomplished *Literature and Western Man* (1960). In his eighties he summed up his life in the following terms:

> I have been on the whole a very lucky man. I have helped to bring up a flourishing healthy family, who always seem glad to see me. My work has gone all over the world. I have been able to write just what I wanted to write and have been handsomely rewarded for it. If I have refused various honours, it is chiefly because my name has been able to stand alone, without any fancy handles to it.
>
> (Priestley 1977: 151)

Career: the politics of the 'new' criticism – Priestley and the modernists

Much of Priestley's autobiographical writing pays witness to his extensive travels in the United States, Egypt and continental Europe. It also reveals his capacity for detailed analyses of other cultures and ways of living (see Priestley 1940, 1946). With his novels and plays published and performed in many languages, he was an international 'bestseller' and a well-known public figure, though not always well liked (Thomson 1986). His practical and intellectual engagement with 'other cultures' facilitated Priestley's ability to comment on world events and to critique modes of behaviour which he saw as counterproductive in terms of their impact on the improvement of the social fabric of life. His class origins and political beliefs set him apart from many of his literary contemporaries, in part because of his explicit insistence on the interrelationship between ideology, politics and the purpose and nature of art.

For Priestley, literary criticism had changed immensely in its intent and purpose after the First World War. In the 1920s and early 1930s the long novel was no longer in favour, either with publishers, for whom it was expensive to produce and market, or with the new critics for whom it lacked the 'modernist' touch. Priestley was viewed negatively by these 'new' critics such as F.R. Leavis, because he was seen as appealing to a middle-brow audience and to a mass market. This audience was the negative side of the 'mass-civilisation/minority-culture split, diagnosed as the chief condition of cultural ill-health' by the all powerful Leavis, who Priestley, in turn, attacked on a number of occasions (Priestley 1956; Williams and Matthews 1997: 2). John Atkins suggests that Leavis considered himself 'a most important critic', and had nagging at the back of his mind 'the suspicion that Priestley and his kind had a good deal of significance' (Atkins 1981: 268). Literary and cultural critic John Carey (1992) has pointed to the modernist cultural anxiety about the 'masses', their growing numbers and increasing role as consumers in an emergent commodified culture. For Carey, the modernists did not wish art to be a mass affair, he even goes so far as to suggest that they wanted art and literature to be inaccessible to the masses, for aesthetics to override any possibilities of empathetic connection. Like Priestley, Carey also notes that the idea of the 'masses', as explored in novels by writers as different as E.M. Forster and Virginia Woolf, was in fact a construct, a way of overcoming cultural anxiety as experienced by the privileged classes, and a response to the gradual democratisation of education and the growth of the media which happened in the early part of the twentieth century (Carey 1992: 8–16; Priestley 1941b). These were social developments which Priestley, albeit with a critical eye, celebrated. Although Carey's views have been critiqued by some as oversimplifying modernist influences on European art, they are views with which Priestley would have had some sympathy. He saw the 'new' critics as 'demonising the objective tone of the great literature of the past', instead, heralding literature which displayed 'an unhealthy obsession with the self and its workings' (Atkins 1981: 263).

> The journalist-critics I knew . . . were rapidly losing that all-important central influence, they were no longer capturing the intellectual young. . . . There was now arriving, to dominate the centre, a new kind of criticism, colder and harder, intolerant in manner, arrogant in tone, and so immediately attractive to intellectual youth, itself intolerant and arrogant. It was theological and absolutist: severe and high priests moved in. Only a small amount of writing, written by and for an elite, was Literature, all else was rubbish. . . . These new critics were like members of a grim little secret society, making out lists of the few who would be allowed to survive, the many who must be assassinated. As their influence grew, I was out-of-date before I even began. . . . What was produced by the extrovert, facing the outer world, was simply so much popular entertainment, not Literature at all . . . the qualities looked for and most highly regarded were originality, strangeness and intensity . . . what no longer counted . . . were breadth and vitality.
>
> (Priestley 1962: 153–4)

Indeed his analysis that he was seen as some kind of 'Quisling of letters. No longer a man and a brother . . . "a best seller"' (Priestley 1962: 184), is borne out by Virginia Woolf's famous condemnation of him as a 'tradesman of letters'.

> At the age of 50 Priestley will be saying 'Why don't the highbrows admire me? It isn't true that I only write for money.' He will be enormously rich; but there will be that thorn in his shoe – or so I hope. Yet I have not read, & I daresay shall never read, a book by Priestley. . . . And I invent this phrase for Bennett & Priestley 'the tradesman of letters'.
>
> (Bell 1980: 318)

Woolf's gleeful dismissal of Priestley, whose work she non-chalantly admits to never having read, is indicative both of class snobbery and of what Priestley identified as the ready position of the new critics to undermine writers whose work gained popularity in a growing market. Woolf's diaries, ironically, are full of details about how much she earned from reviewing and criticism, and she often notes the number of her books sold, pleased that her name is getting known (Bell 1980: 149). Such hostilities, as expressed by Woolf, originated in both class and professional snobbery as much as any kind of hardline position on the aesthetics of literature. Priestley's son Tom, a film and documentary maker, has suggested that in fact Priestley was persistently the victim of critical social snobbery and this, in effect, matches John Carey's analysis of the new criticism.[6] For Priestley, however, it was more to do with suffering from the 'fixed idea, itself an indictment of our whole culture, that anything widely popular must necessarily be bad. . . . Sales figures criticism is simply a fraud' (Priestley 1962: 184): he felt that he was 'too conventional for the *avant-garde*, too experimental for Aunt Edna' – that his work was critically viewed as being somehow too populist for the elite yet too impenetrable for 'ordinary' folk (Priestley 1962: 225–6).

Clearly, Priestley's critical reception as a novelist was influenced by factors beyond the texts themselves. The 'new critics' were keen on the emerging modernist aesthetic which demanded a new literature after 1918. The majority of this 'new' literature came in large part from a social class to which Priestley did not belong. He was a professional writer and an intellectual but there were real financial implications to his professional activity; he had no family money to fall back on should he fail to get published. In retrospect, however, Priestley had more in common with the modernists than the contemporary critique of his work suggests; a strong sense of the urban/rural divide, an interest in the idea and experience of time (see Levenson 2004), a desire to experiment with form – especially in theatre – and a repeated investigation of the psyche and so on. He was also completely au fait with developments in European literature and theatre, as is evidenced by his wide-ranging intellectual work, *Literature and Western*

Man (1960). In fact, it is in this book that he best sums up his attitude to the modernist phase:

> The truth is that . . . the relative view is still the more sensible, impatient dichotomies are still unjustified and misleading. People cannot be either justly or profitably divided . . . into art-takers and art-refusers, into readers of Literature and consumers of trash, into the *élite* and the masses.
>
> (Priestley 1960: 331)

For Priestley the function and social reach of literature in the 1920s and 1930s had changed, not only because of increased leisure time among working people but also because of developments in media which catered more to the visual senses, such as film. This was not a criticism of film per se – he even suggests that Charlie Chaplin brought to film the humour which Dickens had brought to literature and praised his powers of social observation and expression (Priestley 1940: 194) – rather, that the post First World War generation was the first for whom visual stimulus was the dominant mode (Priestley 1960: 332). Literature clearly had a new role, but Priestley felt that the modernists lacked the appropriate level of social analysis and worked to limited notions of what constituted literature. He considered Virginia Woolf, much of whose criticism and prose he admired, to be absorbed by her own 'absolutist intolerant theory' predicated on internal dialogue and self-absorption (Priestley 1960: 426), and argued that those who were trying to be 'poetic' in the theatre – such as Christopher Fry, W.H. Auden and T.S. Eliot – were not interested or knowledgeable enough about the pragmatics of theatre. The dynamics of live theatre production had to be prioritised over the desire to be poetic. Thus, in critiquing Sean O'Casey's *Oak Leaves and Lavender* (1946), Priestley felt that O'Casey's form, 'a kind of verbal opera', where we are left with the 'Opera without the orchestra', meant that the dramatic action was lost, that the poetic form did not work as stage dialogue.[7] According to Priestley, T.S. Eliot had almost solved this problem with *The Family Reunion* (1939), which Priestley's production company, the London Mask Theatre, had produced in 1939, but here, again, the poetic language did not work well in the theatre, and for Priestley in theatre, 'a miss is a good as a mile'.[8]

Thus, Priestley often worked against the interwar literary and academic critics who were concerned with defining the literature of their generation in terms of a modernist aesthetic. He battled with them in the press and in his other writings: he believed that literature could educate and enlighten, but that it was also there to be enjoyed, and to reflect on the human condition in a fast changing culture.

Politics: the politics of class and social action

For Priestley the speed of technological change, and its effect on the populace so shocked by the events of the First World War, was not mirrored by real social change in terms of the class structures which had so dominated British society before the war. Just as an analysis of class difference lies, to some extent, at the root of the barrage of academic criticism aimed at Priestley as a writer, so too he saw that the entrenchment of the class system in the fabric of English life, had not been destroyed by the war to the level that many had hoped it would be (see McKibbin 2000).

Letter to a Returning Serviceman (1945) is predicated on a comparative analysis of the social and private world to which Priestley had returned as a young man after the First World War, and that of the immediate post Second World War, a war in which he was too old to fight. Written to an imaginary returning soldier 'Robert', Priestley critiques the way in which the post First World War national press and the government tried to persuade the 'reformer, the revolutionary . . . who said there must be no more of this murderous nonsense', that he could in fact relax, that no such war would ever happen again (Priestley 1945b: 4). Of course, they were wrong and Priestley tries to encourage the 'returning soldier' to keep a wary eye on social policy and political rhetoric now that the Second World War is over.

> There was a time around 1940, when we were able to convince a lot of people that only a diseased and rotten society

could have thrown up a Hitler, but since then there has been a huge campaign telling us day and night that it was Hitler who somehow produced, presumably from his box of watercolours, any disease and rottenness there may be in our society. Tory gentlemen who have clearly not learned anything, and now never will, confidently offer themselves as our guardians again, assuming that because they choose to forget the sickening muddle, darkening into tragedy, of the Twenties and Thirties, we shall have forgotten too.

(Priestley 1945b: 6)

Priestley notes that although many of the old ruling class were 'living in the past', there were many who still held real political and economic power – the 'tough fellows behind the huge monopolies and cartels, the secret emperors and warlords of finance and industry' (Priestley 1945b: 15). His analysis has a Marxist flavour in terms of its expressed understanding of the interrelationship between the economy, social power and cultural production. He encourages the 'returning serviceman' to have high expectations of his own social worth and ability to change his public world, and to

refuse with scorn the great dope-dreams of the economic emperors and their sorcerers and Hollywood sirens. Don't allow them to inject you with Glamour, Sport, Sensational News, and all the De-luxe nonsense, as if they were filling you with an aesthetic.

(Priestley 1945b: 31)

Priestley's progressive political outlook combined his understanding of the class system with an analysis of power structures and the social propaganda of the political right.

The experienced realities of social inequality during Priestley's time in the army, where the officers, mainly drawn from the aristocracy and ruling classes, maintained their positions of privilege, affirmed his belief that privilege was not to do with wealth. Privilege was tied into an embedded class system which even the circumstances of war could not undermine: 'I served four and a half years in the army, where money does not count for much, and privilege, carefully adjusted according to rank and then very strongly enforced, counts for a lot' (Priestley 1940: 102–3). He criticised George Bernard Shaw for believing that a redistribution of wealth would necessarily produce a more equal society.

> I have heard Bernard Shaw argue eloquently against the smallest inequalities in income, and demonstrate that anything short of genuine equality of pay all round will keep us entangled in this sticky web of money and poison all our relations with one another. But Shaw appears to believe in privilege. And this will not do. He has never lived in a society in which money did not mean much but privilege meant a great deal.
>
> (Priestley 1940: 102–3)

Using the example of a post-revolutionary Russia, he notes that producing a simplified social structure through wealth distribution has not created an 'equal' society; here the old class system has gone only to be replaced by another which is even more 'iron bound' (Priestley 1940). Priestley's belief that the class system and the easy manner in which power had essentially remained in the hands of the few – despite the genuine upheaval of war – underpinned much of his writing and especially his plays. *An Inspector Calls* (1946) or *They Came to a City* (1943) demand of the audience that they consider their own role in the maintenance of the class system and suggests an appraisal of alternative social structures and modes of behaviour. The First World War had created the fantasy that we might get rid of 'feudal Britain for ever, but soon the ranks of privileged persons closed up'. Priestley maintained that we 'are not a democracy, but a plutocracy roughly disguised as an aristocracy' (Priestley 1941a: 224–5).

Although J.B. Priestley was not a 'party man', he sustained a practice of social and political observation and critique in much of his work and his alignment with political causes was varied and complex; his 'voice was prominent amongst those of the radical polemicists' (Thomson 1986: 5). 'Instrumental in the forming and success of CND [the Campaign for Nuclear Disarmament] as a major public protest movement' in 1958 (T. Priestley 1997: 64), Priestley shared the British public's concern with the Conservative government's decision to fund the manufacture of nuclear arms. He wrote and campaigned fervently for CND but resigned after the organisation became established and was run through large and more democratic meetings. According to Diana Collins, another of the organisation's founders, his then wife Jacquetta Hawkes thought Priestley a 'great resigner' (Collins 1994: 23). He writes very little about the specifics of his campaign work in his autobiographies, either for theatre organisations such as the International Theatre Conference or the International Theatre Institute or for 'leftist' groups like the 1941 Committee (Waters 1994: 220). Similarly neither he nor his biographers mention his work as one of the founding members for the Homosexual Law Reform Society (HLRS) and its charitable wing, the Albany Trust. The HLRS had been set up in 1958 as a direct result of the 1957 Wolfenden Report, a government commissioned report which called for a liberalisation of the laws discriminating against homosexuals (Weeks 1990: 165–8). The first meetings had been held in Priestley's London flat at The Albany in central London.

Dan Rebellato, however, notes Priestley's hostility to homosexuals in his attacks on the way in which the London theatre industry was run (Rebellato 1999: 184–5; see also Priestley 1947b: 53). It is clear that Priestley felt the criminalising of homosexuality created a kind of ghetto community and in the theatre, a secret society which 'enthusiastically gives its praise and patronage to whatever is decorative, "amusing", "good theatre", witty in the right way, and likely to make heterosexual relationships look ridiculous' (Priestley 1953: 516). Alan Sinfield (1999) also categorises Priestley as among those who perceived the theatrical and literary worlds of the interwar period as being dominated by discreet 'leisure class homosexuals' and suggests that his 'nononsense, working class attitude to sexuality' often meant 'misogyny and homophobia' (Sinfield 1999: 255). There is, however, nothing even mildly misogynistic in Priestley's theatre writing. His assaults on the theatre industry were more frequently focused on a critique of its structure, the concentration of ownership and the attitude of the state to the arts in general: he continually attacked the system and individuals he saw as responsible for its maintenance. His work for the Albany Trust was inspired by more than a simple desire to change the nature of what was or was not being put on in the London theatres. His association with the organisation signifies a craving, at a time when any argument for gay rights could cause serious damage to his public image, for real legalistic change that would bring about social change. Priestley's social action was driven by his beliefs in social equality and human rights; homosexuals are part of the variety of society and should not be stigmatised so that they have to live somehow outside of it.

Priestley was involved in numerous political organisations and for each he wrote and publicised their causes: that he never stayed as part of those organisations for long should not undermine the dedication with which he approached their needs. Just as his personality and career were complex and multilayered, so too were the ways in which he expressed his deepening but constantly developing beliefs. His marriages, to a childhood neighbour Pat Tempest, to Jane Bannerman, an upper-middle-class society hostess with a deep social conscience, and finally to intellectual and social reformer Jacquetta Hawkes, coincide with the stages of development of his own personal beliefs and professional needs. Similarly, his political beliefs developed, deepened and became more strongly enveloped in his thinking about the human psyche as his career progressed.

Life, career, politics: conclusion

Readings of Priestley's life, career and politics themselves often reveal certain social and academic prejudices rather than 'truth'. From northern lower-middle-class roots, he ended up living a life seen by some as the 'epitome of dignified luxury' (Willis 1991: 12). For some his genuine intellectual capacities and concern for social justice, were often undermined by a 'deliberate reversion to small-town hard-headedness' (Ustinov 1979: 313). Equally contradictory, some biographies refer to his extra-marital affairs at the same time as focusing on the emotional depth and domestic complexities of his marriages and dedication to his familial relationships. He was a key twentieth century playwright, a fact recognised by the industry but not by the academy, for whom the mid-twentieth century British theatre has been traditionally seen as commercialised and lacking invention. John Baxendale suggests that literary analyses have, toward the end of the twentieth century, reflected those of the elite 'modernist' tradition, in locating Priestley as old fashioned and somehow reactionary (Baxendale 2001). What is evident, however, is that analyses of Priestley's oeuvre have suffered from changing trends in intellectual and critical discourse. Thus the question asked at the beginning of Baxendale's appraisal of Priestley's work on 'Englishness', namely, 'what has posterity done with J.B. Priestley?', is a pertinent one. The overriding evidence, however, is that whatever position the critics and intellectuals have taken historically, Priestley's plays and novels continue to sell. Each year sees a significant number of productions of his plays, in both professional and amateur theatres all over the world: more recently, Stephen Daldry's extraordinarily long running revival of *An Inspector Calls* (1992) has become a significant cultural phenomenon. What is clear is that there is no other British playwright of his generation who engaged so deeply with the dynamics of cultural production and the function and practice of theatre.

2 The function and practice of theatre
Visions, theories and critical responses

> I did not go to work in the Theatre and then discover, because it helped me to earn a living, that Theatre is important. I left other kinds of writing, which offered me a safe living and far more peace of mind . . . because I believed the Theatre to be important. And more than once . . . I have told myself that I would write no more for the Theatre, would compete no longer in its nightmare obstacle race, but always I have returned because I have never been able to rid myself of the conviction that the Theatre, representing the communal art of drama, was far more important, far more deeply significant, than most people ever imagined.
>
> (Priestley 1947b: 69–70)

A 'constant playgoer during his 'teens in Bradford' (Priestley 1970: 156), and finding solace as a young soldier in the garrison theatre run by Basil Dean during the First World War in France (Priestley 1941c: 26–8), theatre had played a significant role in Priestley's life from an early age.[1] His view in the opening years of the Second World War, that actors could 'serve' their country as entertainers as opposed to soldiers, during times of conflict, bears witness to his belief that theatre had a very real social function. Priestley's belief in theatre is a 'communal art', deeply 'significant' both in social and psychological terms, is one which underpins the majority of his writing on theatre, both as practice and as a form of cultural production.

Priestley wrote a great deal about theatre, both factual and fictional and his theories and observations embraced a wide spectrum of actual practice: he loved the 'popular' theatre of the metropolitan and provincial music halls and variety stages. He was also as familiar with theatrical activity in Europe and the United States as he was with theatre in England. Priestley wrote both critically and with affection about clowns and stand-up performers as well as actors (Priestley 1975, 1976), but noted in the late 1920s that variety theatre had somewhat lost its edge (Priestley 1928: 161). Similarly, when in 1928 he writes about an experience of visiting a touring show in the provinces, he not only gently mocks the outdated appearance of the performances and the simplicity of presentation, but also asserts that such shows are part of the richness of the theatre experience and must not be lost to progress or modernisation. Of the lead actress's stage exit at the end of her performance he notes:

> When she swept out, you could have sworn that the black night had already swallowed her; it was absurd to think that she was behind that little curtain, having a nip of something and keeping her eye on the takings. If her patrons do not rally around her (and I can promise for one), then Drama is dead.
> (Priestley 1928: 161)

Progressive in his era, Priestley celebrated theatre as a unique *live* art, the qualities of which could not be replaced by film or later, by television, a new medium unsuitable to providing an 'imitation of something better done elsewhere' (Priestley 1955: 21). Equally, he saw drama as a component of a live art *form*, not as literature. For Priestley, the actual live production of plays was dependent, first, upon the economic dynamics and structure of a highly commercialised and insular theatre industry, and second, on a largely 'academic' tradition of criticism that supposed drama should appeal more to a 'highbrow' audience.

> The art of drama, as actually presented on the stage, is not a collection of bits and pieces from the other arts, but another kind of art, not very pure perhaps, messy and a trifle vulgar

no doubt, but existing in its own right. This is something that many critics . . . do not seem to understand . . . [they sometimes feel that] Theatre could be raised to a far higher level of achievement if only our poets would write for it.

(Priestley 1947b: 71)

For Priestley, as for practitioners from previous generations such as Granville Barker (see Luckhurst 2006: 78–108), British theatre was being undermined not so much by cinema or alternative forms of entertainment, but by a commercial management system which lacked belief in its value either as an art form or as an inherently necessary form of social and educational activity.

Function: the theatre as an industry

I do not . . . object to the so-called 'commercial manager' as such, although . . . I believe that a large section of the Theatre should be taken out of the control of commercial managements . . . a man cannot produce plays as if he were merely manufacturing hairpins.

(Priestley 1947b: 18)

Unlike the majority of its European counterparts, the British theatre received no real subsidy until after the Second World War, with the formation first of CEMA (Council for Encouragement of Music and the Arts) and then the Arts Council of England in the mid-1940s. British theatre in the first half of the twentieth century was a many-layered industry, largely framed by its commercial status. The industry included provincial theatres, variety venues, London and West End theatres as well as privately run subscription and club theatres – the independent sector (see Davies 1987; Gale 1996, 2004a, 2004b; Marshall 1948). Productions of new plays were usually funded by investors and backers, often premiered or 'tried out' outside London and then brought into a London venue. It was the economic possibilities of a production of a play which drove investment, just as in the 'popular' theatre, stage acts which pulled the crowds were the ones that got rebooked. The British theatre of this period was driven largely by market forces and this was something which Priestley, along with other playwrights who had gone before him, like Granville Barker and G.B. Shaw, objected to (see Kennedy 1989). Priestley joined the well-established line of playwrights who called for some kind of 'national theatre' rather than have the industry run by managements with predominantly economic as opposed to artistic interests.

Tracy C. Davis has remarked that although the 'entertainment industry was so radically altered by the outbreak of war in 1914, many businesses experienced difficulty on the home front' before the war. She notes G.B. Shaw's view that the popularity of 'non-legitimate theatre' – the music halls and associated entertainment venues – represented 'consumer choice' (Davis 2000: 354). Equally, from the late Edwardian period onwards, the picture palaces – home of early cinema – began to take up a significant part of the market. The film industry based its model of distribution and the circulation of its products on that of the theatre industry, and so could capitalise on ready made systems of touring and attracting audiences (Davis 2000: 359). Priestley recognised the importance of film as a possible usurper to theatre, but felt that the economic position of the British theatre system was more the result of poor organisation and a concentration in managerial power, than it was related to the popularity of film. West End theatres, by the end of the interwar period, were almost entirely owned and run by a small and tightly knit management cartel. Often referred to as the Group, this cartel of companies had, by the 1940s, manoeuvred themselves into a position where they either owned or ran most of the profitable theatres in London. Members of one company often sat on the managerial boards of another and so the perception of a monopoly was not unfounded. These owner/managers produced large-scale musical comedies and revues as well as plays and so held power over all quarters of the entertainment industry. Unlike the pre-1914 period, most of the owner/managers were not actors or 'theatre people' but rather, investors and business people. Where the Victorian West End was dominated – not always unproblematically so – by actor-managers, such as Beerbohm Tree or Henry Irving, the post 1914 period saw theatres moving outside the field of artist-led management. There are only a few exceptions to this, such as Gladys Cooper and Frank Curzon's management of the Playhouse and Gerald du Maurier's at Wyndham's (see Morley 1979) or the independent and privately run club and subscription theatres like the Everyman in Hampstead, Lena Ashwell's Century Theatre in Notting Hill and the Embassy in Swiss Cottage. These latter organisations were essentially privately run and made little profit unless productions transferred into the West End.

Priestley was one of many who warned of the impact of 'the activities of speculating middlemen, who bought up theatre leases with the object of re-letting at a profit to the producing managements' (Sandison 1953: 52). From 1914 onwards London theatre buildings had become valuable real estate in an economy where the value of land and buildings in central London had risen significantly. Priestley recognised that the mainstream theatre was an industry open to all who had the financial resources; that the 'horizontal and vertical combination' of an industry operating at this level (Sandison 1953: 52), meant that the means of production had been largely removed from the control of those who worked within the theatre itself.

> Theatre at present is not controlled by dramatists, actors, producers or managers, but chiefly by theatre owners, men of property who may or may not have a taste for the drama. The owners . . . take too much out of the Theatre. . . . What I condemn is the property system that allows public amenities and a communal art to be controlled by persons who happen to be rich enough to acquire playhouses.
>
> (Priestley 1947b: 6)

Priestley's assessment of the impact of this form of management drove him to form his own small production company, the practicalities of which are examined later in this chapter. But he also understood the complexities of, and was deeply concerned by, this style of investment in cultural assets.

> In the West End . . . the producing manager guarantees the theatre owner a weekly minimum that covers all the owner's

charges and expenses, but over and above that the owner takes a substantial share of the returns. Thus if the production is a big success, the theatre owner (who has taken no risk) receives a fat slice of the profits. Clearly for the owner this is gambling without losing. . . . It stands to reason that only desperate men – and the producing manager is a desperate man these days – would accept such monstrous terms. But in many West End theatres now, the producing manager pays the salaries . . . and expenses . . . a proportion of the managerial expenses out of a share of the weekly returns that amounts to 55 per cent . . . as things are at present, the theatre-owner (or as often happens, the gang of speculators who have moved in to secure leases) risks nothing and contributes nothing, and marches off with most of the profit.

(Priestley 1947b: 29–30)

The managements and theatre owners received the financial benefit of theatrical production from the initial rental and payment of recurrent costs, and from their agreed percentage of box office sales, regardless of any profit gained from the production. It was the production company, not the building owners, who stood to lose out if a production was unsuccessful. As a result many productions were withdrawn because the short-term potential profit margin was not high enough; there were plenty of potential new productions waiting for a theatre venue.

Priestley also campaigned against the taxation of theatrical productions, which impacted on the production managements, not the building owners. The Entertainment Tax, initiated in 1916 as a wartime emergency, was applied to box office receipts, not overall profit: the government earned from a production even if the production management lost money. In 1924 the tax was abolished on cheaper seats, those under the price of 1s 3d (6 pence), but this benefited the cinema more than the theatre, where seats were costed at a higher rate. By 1942, the tax was levied at 33.3 per cent. The amateur and privately run independent theatres were exempt from this form of taxation, just as they were from the official censorship of the Lord Chamberlain's office imposed on 'public' theatres and so could experiment more freely (Gale

1996; Nicholson 2003, 2005). Interestingly, the West End relied on their ethos of experimentation and profited from its successes. As Norman Marshall noted in 1948, 'It is astonishing how few . . . West End successes, apart from musicals, farces and thrillers were originally created by West End managers' (Marshall 1948: 14–16). Noël Coward was one among many who had their early work produced by a private/independent theatre, with the Everyman's production of *The Vortex* in 1924, and it was often smaller production managements, like Basil Dean's ReandeaN Productions, which took risks with new writers such as Clemence Dane, in the 1920s (see Gale 2005). Such speculative attitudes to production were less likely by the 1950s, although companies such as the new English Stage Company at the Royal Court theatre could receive funding from the Arts Council and so be less commercially oriented (see Roberts 1999).

Priestley's critique of the way the theatre industry was being run focused on the lack of impetus for the owning management cartels to invest in new writers or in innovation. They could profit financially from simply leasing their buildings and artistically from the tax-free status of the independent sector, which sustained itself through the dedication of a minority to developing new writers and new forms. West End theatres could often earn more money than they originally cost to build, but it was the owners of the real estate who profited from this not the theatre artists (Priestley 1947b: 27).

For Priestley the government was negligent in maintaining the imposition of the Entertainment Tax at such a high levy. He pointed to the fact that the cinema industry benefited from the terms of this taxation: it paid lower levels of tax but the theatre provided a training ground for actors and bore the brunt of the costs for new plays, successful ones of which were often adapted for the cinema. Priestley was not against the cinema; he often defended it as popular entertainment, feeling that it 'needed defence . . . because many intellectuals wrongly attacked [it] sometimes showing far less wisdom and sensitiveness than the ordinary man' (Priestley 1940: 239). He was, however, critical of the film industry as epitomised by Hollywood, noting rather prophetically that the new celebrity film culture meant that the 'head of Metro Goldwyn Mayer will soon seem much more important than the president himself. The great questions will suddenly change their form if not their urgency. Will Chaplin finish his new picture? Has Garbo retired to Switzerland?' (Priestley 1940: 177). Both the emergent film industries and celebrity cultures in Britain and North America were reliant on their respective theatre industries, especially during the 1920s and 1930s, and yet they had no real economic relationship with them; cinema benefited from theatre but it was rarely a reciprocal arrangement.

Priestley's criticism of the management and economics of the theatre industry can be divided into three key areas: first, the monopoly of ownership and its impact on what was or was not produced; second, the refusal of the state, in setting taxation levels, to take into account the cost of production; third, the refusal of the state to differentiate appropriately between the theatre and the cinema in terms of levels of taxation – cinema seats were cheap by comparison and so mostly untaxed by 1924. He stressed that the state benefited from an art form in which it declined to invest. Theatre was a national asset, a 'communal art' which required nurturing and support:

> the system . . . is all wrong . . . gambling has taken the place of policy . . . this private commercial enterprise in the Theatre . . . builds up no new loyalties, shows itself incapable of sensible planning, and largely creates a feeling of insecurity and uncertainty.
>
> (Priestley 1947b: 36–9)

The emphasis and focus of criticism varied at different points in his career, but still in the late 1940s, he suggested that the theatre needed to organise itself more effectively, and challenged the lack of substantial funding for drama during the early years of the Arts Council: drama received 30 per cent of the total funding awarded to music in 1944–5 (Priestley 1947b: 23).

The fact that after the Second World War rents had risen further and fewer theatres were operational, meant that the 'long run' system was even more problematic than it had been before the war.

For Priestley, the long run system whereby productions of plays which had made a strong initial impact were kept running, because they continued to make a steady profit for the management, inhibited the development of actors and playwrights alike. As others pointed out, 'each long run in the West End means a potential market lost' (Richards 1931: 231), and for Priestley this meant that not only did the actors' performances become stale and complacent, but also theatre buildings were tied into productions where even at 50 per cent audience capacity, profit could be made.

> Suppose . . . a play . . . opens in a theatre that is not expensive to run. It is not a great success; it is not a failure; and for some time it just 'ticks over', neither making much money nor losing much. If such a play can be kept going for a year or so . . . then after that it begins to acquire a prestige and a momentum as a long-run play . . . it will achieve a reputation and be talked about . . . until it becomes one of the productions that every visitor must try to see . . . and then the box-office manager . . . finds himself selling out the house night after night, week after week, month after month. And the visitors pack in to see a mechanical performance, long stereotyped . . . of a second-rate little piece, and then wonder why they are disappointed. . . . No production is worth seeing after it has been running, without a break, for a year.
>
> (Priestley 1947b: 21–2)

Function: theatre and community

Priestley maintained that theatre had the power to educate and to integrate and enliven a community, to help it to think through the social issues which affected it. Such idealistic expectations drove his theatre work. Statistics verify his experience of the impact of the profit-oriented long run system; while the period after 1918 to the mid-1930s saw a periodical increase in the number of new plays going into production, by the late 1940s and early 1950s a higher percentage were running for longer. Equally, by this time the ownership and management of theatres was concentrated and fewer new plays were going into production.

Priestley felt that audiences were being cheated, that what they were given as entertainment did not reflect the wealth of talent available. In the late 1940s he stated:

> the economic conditions of theatrical production are appalling, and all the old faults of the English Theatre are strongly in evidence. We are better off because we have created new audiences with a sharp appetite for good drama, and directors, players, and designers are crying out for serious work, and young playwrights by the dozen are dipping or chewing their pens. It is, some of us feel, *Now or Never* for the English Theatre.
>
> (Priestley 1947b: 14)

The notion that the theatre was in crisis, that certain sections of the industry should be pulled out of commercial and into some sort of state management, was an echo of debates in the nineteenth century. What Priestley believed, however, was that English audiences had been let down by a theatre production system that prioritised the potential to make money over the nurturing of new playwrights and established playwrights whose work was popular but not 'star vehicle' material. For him the 'English character' was at once untheatrical in its outward habits yet had playgoing 'at a deeper and more instinctive level of behaviour than it is with most peoples' (Priestley 1947b: 16). The state supported other arts and built museums and galleries but the theatre 'which is far closer to our people than the visual arts', received little patronage of this sort (Priestley 1947b: 17). He saw the structure and management of the continental theatre as a possible model which could be adopted in England; here drama was treated as a 'serious and important communal activity' (Priestley 1947b: 18). Priestley not only blamed the commercial managements, the press and the ruling classes for limiting the possibilities of drama within the industry, but also was less than complimentary about audiences who saw theatre as 'a hazy muddle of "show business", a vague lucky dip, out of which a few fascinating and glamorous personalities are fortunate enough to pluck glittering "success"'

(Priestley 1947b: 52). He felt that just as Edwardian audiences had 'fitted in a visit to a play as part of an evening's entertainment' (Priestley 1970: 155), so too, some audiences during the interwar period and into the 1950s went to theatre in order to participate vicariously in a celebrity world.

Unusual in the amount of his own work which was produced in theatres abroad, Priestley often berated the fact that serious continental drama did not find its way onto West End stages often enough despite British plays often transferring well in foreign countries. The assertion that drama is embedded in a communal identity in most of continental Europe is a recurrent theme in a great deal of Priestley's theorising on theatre. He praised the way in which the community oriented amateur theatre, 'from terrifying superior persons, producing T.S. Eliot in exquisite little theatres, to village dames and damsels giggling over their scripts in rural Institutes', challenged the professional theatre through the quality of its work and the kinds of work it chose to produce. It was in fact here that one often found productions of foreign plays (Priestley 1947b: 51). Like the best continental subsidised theatres, the best amateur theatre was thriving and various, frequently experimented, and yet found a consistent and dedicated audience: 'there are towns so filled with busy amateur players that the visiting professionals are starved of audiences' (Priestley 1947b: 51). Priestley even went so far as to suggest that we should try to create a theatre in which 'it ought to be easy to be a bright young amateur this year and a hopeful professional the next' (Priestley 1947b: 68). His criticism of sections of the amateur theatre was that it tried to ape what it perceived as 'professional practice' rather than playing to its own strengths, and that it appeared disorganised and directionless. This was also his criticism of the British theatre as a whole, that it was plagued by economic instability and a lack of sense of its own place in society. He wanted a theatre culture where workers would feel, 'that they themselves are good and valuable citizens, that the Theatre is not something existing precariously on the edge of the community, but it is set squarely inside it, in an honoured position' (Priestley 1947b: 52–3).

Vision: fictional theatre – Priestley's 'theatre novels'

Priestley's attacks on the theatre industry aroused the suspicion of 'educational experts' and 'official bigwigs' (Priestley 1947b: 69), but he insisted that we have to

> see the theatre as something much more than a superior substitute for the reading of dramatic literature. We have to prove that it is valuable and unique, that it does something supremely well worth doing, and that nothing else can take its place.
>
> (Priestley 1947b: 70)

Among the playwrights of his generation, he was unusual in that he genuinely took up the challenge of trying to change the ways in which the industry might be run. On the one hand he played on the idea that there was something almost magical about theatre, that the whole was equal to more than the sum of its parts. On the other hand, he proposed very pragmatic solutions to the problems of organisation and economics. Ambitious in taking on such a huge industry Priestley saw theatre's potential to create equality and a sense of belonging to a community.

> There is no more enchanting box of tricks in the world than a theatre, especially a theatre that makes its own scenery and costumes. . . . You all start together on a new level, and come away from it feeling refreshed, as one does when that curse of our English life – our class system – has been temporarily removed. *The Theatre and You*, 1938.
>
> (quoted in Priestley 2005: 9)

The vision of a theatre which contributes to and belongs to a community as well as offering opportunities for artistic expression, is present in Priestley's numerous 'theatre novels'. In works such as *The Good Companions* (1929), *Jenny Villiers* (1947) and *Lost Empires* (1965) Priestley uses theatre and performance as a central focal point in narratives driven by themes such as community, human connectivity, memory and loss. *The Good Companions* is examined later in this volume (see Chapter 6), but its story – of people from different classes and social backgrounds, being brought together through their engagement with theatre – resonates with his ideas about the ways in which theatre has the power to make humans connect emotionally and practically, in a precarious post-war world.

Lost Empires (1965), written relatively late in Priestley's career, sees Richard Herncastle join his uncle, an inventive and admired stage illusionist famous for his Indian Magician Act, on a tour of the music halls and variety stages immediately before the First World War. Herncastle's journey takes the reader through rehearsals and band calls, through the process of working out new illusions to amaze the audience, through the trials of touring, life in theatrical digs, backstage crime, love affairs and so on. By the end of the novel, Herncastle has left the theatre to join the army, and so the first stage of his right of passage ends, to be replaced by the hardship of war. Underpinning the novel is a desire to narrativise the theatre as a community in and of itself, but also to de-romanticise the processes involved in performance. Through using the pre-war setting, Priestley expresses a critical nostalgia toward the Edwardian period, rather than returning us to an idealised 'cosy England' (Baxendale 2001). As with *An Inspector Calls* (see Chapter 7) the return to this historical moment is a device for social criticism (Braine 1978: 145).

Lost Empires was adapted for the stage by Keith Waterhouse and Willis Hall in 1974. The York Theatre Royal production was performed as a musical and divided into two acts of eleven and eight scenes respectively. Of the nineteen scenes, eighteen have different locations, and of these ten are theatre spaces ranging from backstage, onstage and in the scene dock of six different theatres. The Waterhouse/Willis production, performed by a combined company from the Cambridge Touring Theatre and the Birmingham Repertory, played on a cultural fascination with the process of theatre making as well as the original novel's swift movement from one theatre-related location to another, shifting from the Theatre pub scene to the stage and backstage of the Glasgow Empire in Act I to the scene dock, London digs and the

Finsbury Park Empire in Act II. An expensive show to produce, it was predicated on a form of nostalgia among British audiences as reflected in the popularity of television programmes like *The Good Old Days* in the 1970s. Produced as part of the BBC's Light Entertainment programming on and off from 1953 to the mid-1980s. *The Good Old Days* aimed to replicate, albeit in a somewhat sterilised manner, the vitality of the Victorian and Edwardian music hall.

Later, Laurence Olivier and Colin Firth starred in Granada Television's lavish 1986 production of *Lost Empires*, which was also successfully distributed in North America (Nown 1986).[2] The television adaptation centralises the importance of Richard Herncastle's emotional and sexual journey; both his experiences on the frontline trenches and in the variety theatres of Edwardian England serve as the foundations on which his 'coming of age' is built.

The stage and television versions used different dominant themes in their adaptations of the original Priestley novel: the stage version exploits the appeal of theatrical spaces – those associated with public performance, and those, such as the backstage areas, associated with the processes of performance – using the musical form as framing device. The television adaptation focuses on creating an authentic replication of Edwardian variety performer/audience experience, as the background in which Richard Herncastle's journey from innocence to 'manhood' takes place. Neither therefore makes any attempt to remain absolutely 'true' to the novel, but both take from it a preoccupation with a nostalgic theatrical space and the demystification of the processes of theatre in terms of community and the everyday.

Priestley's unpublished novel, with the working title of *These Our Actors*, which he began in 1939, shares with *Lost Empires* an emphasis on the fictionalised experience of making performance.[3] The novel is set in the Birmanpool Repertory Theatre (a thinly disguised referent to Birmingham and Liverpool repertory theatres), with Miss Padbury as the business manager – another thinly disguised referent, this time to the philanthropic West Midland's Quaker Cadbury family. Priestley signifies a particular form of English theatrical activity which was becoming almost financially untenable by the time he began the novel. The English Repertory theatres had blossomed during the early part of the century, but by 1939, there were comparatively few left. These theatres provided training grounds for actors as well as a steady flow of productions of plays for regional audiences. Some, such as Birmingham and the Gaiety and Rusholme Repertory in Manchester, were more experimental in their choice of repertoire, promoting the work, both on their home ground and on tour, of new playwrights and experimenting with production techniques (see Gardner 2004; Rowell and Jackson 1984).

The depiction of the Birmanpool Repertory Theatre is one of a theatre in decline, a theatre in a 'bleak wilderness of aldermen, manufacturers and dubious non-conformist parsons' (Priestley c.1939a: 8). In contrast, Humphrey Pike, the newly employed leading actor, still believes in the 'magical' possibilities of theatre. Again, there is a focus on process, as Pike deconstructs the experience of rehearsal.

> Two things about rehearsal that are wonderful. First, you're seeing something brought to life – all shaped and coloured and fixed up to the last detail . . . and the second reason why rehearsals are exciting to people with any imagination is that they represent a bit of secret magic. . . . Behind the closed doors and blank face of the theatre you're shaping and colouring and bringing something to life . . . when you're done and the doors are open some . . . will come . . . and that bit of magic will get to work on them.
>
> (Priestley c.1939a: 24)

Pike also points out, however, that when the play is over the 'glimpse of magic' the audience has experienced in the auditorium is 'all that the theatre can give them' (Priestley c.1939a: 38): those in search of magic backstage after the performance will find only the actors removing their make-up. Pike believes in a kind of 'ethics for the performer', whereby rather than play on the audience's expectations of the 'theatrical' and produce stereotyped performances, an actor must continually strive to find both a depth and freshness in their performance. This is very similar to

Priestley's depiction of Jenny Villiers in his 1947 novel of the same name.

Produced as a play in 1946 under the joint sponsorship of the Arts Council, the Old Vic and the Sadler's Wells Trust, at the Theatre Royal in Bath on 13 March 1946, *Jenny Villiers: A ghost story of the theatre* ran for two weeks with a cast which included Patrick Troughton, Pamela Brown and Yvonne Mitchell. The play was scheduled for productions in Norway and Denmark and under consideration for production by Alexander Tairov at the Kamerny Theatre in Moscow.[4] *Jenny Villiers* did not find a London production and was then published as a novel in 1947. Relatively few of Priestley's biographers or literary commentators mention the novel which, as Atkins (1981) points out, is rather odd because of its use of dream and time shift sequences.

The novel's hero/antihero is Martin Cheveril,

> an aging and embittered playwright, who saw the theatre as inevitably rushing towards its own extinction [and] recovers his faith through his encounters with two hopeful young actresses one whom he meets in the flesh and the other whom he meets through a vagary in the time scheme.
>
> (Atkins 1981: 163)

Cheveril, whose *The Glass Door* is being staged in a regional theatre before its London transfer, is under pressure to rewrite sections of the play. His response is that the play is a 'serious attempt to write about the world as it is and people as they actually are' (Priestley 1947a: 8), and so the last act is more pessimistic and 'desolate' than the producers would like. His leading actress does not share his pessimism about theatre which she feels is always 'renewing its enchantment' (Priestley 1947a: 6), and is shocked at his statement that the theatre 'as we know it', will not

> last much longer. The old witchcraft's just about wearing out . . . I know it has always been about to die. But don't forget that most obstinate old invalids do at last turn their faces to the wall. And I believe that's what the Theatre is doing.
>
> (Priestley 1947a: 18)

The actress accuses him of being spoilt by success and leaves him to brood over the rewrites in the theatre green room. What then follows are a series of dream and timeshift sequences in which Cheveril plays witness to the comings and goings of a theatre company working at the same theatre during the 1840s. Cheveril's interest in theatre and the processes of theatre making is reignited through meeting a young actress, Jenny Villiers, who wants to find some kind of 'emotional truth' on stage through 'will, discipline' and 'earnest application' which Priestley himself later identified, as had Stanislavski before him, as being at the centre of the high achieving actors' practice (Priestley 1973: 43). Cheveril remembers the reinvigorating qualities of 'human effort and magic', a combination which Atkins sees as bringing together the 'strands' of that which Priestley considered to be the 'wonder of the Theatre' (Atkins 1981: 164). Cheveril suggests:

> the whole business is symbolic, and . . . unconsciously we all recognise that fact . . . in Theatre . . . character make-up and props are only a shadow show . . . put away when the performance is over . . . what is real, indestructible and enduring is . . . the innermost and deepest feelings – the way an artist sees his work – the root and heart of a real personal relationship – the flame . . . burning clear . . . for all our vulgar mess of paint and canvas and lights and advertisement, we who work in the Theatre . . . because it is a living symbol of the mystery of life, we help to guard and to show the flame.
> (Priestley 1947a: 185–6; see also Priestley 2005: 5)

The themes of 'human effort and magic', of community spirit and the application of unique human skill are prevalent in all Priestley's novels in which theatre and performance feature as a narrative framework. He makes frequent use of the dynamics of history and shifting trends in theatre and performance practice as frameworks for these 'theatre' novels. Although 'theatre as a living symbol for the mystery of life' seems far removed from Priestley's more politically driven analyses of the state of theatre, it lies at the root of much of his writing on the subject: the notion of theatre as somehow 'magical', potentially transformative and communal, is combined with a pragmatic approach to a vision of the ways in which the theatre industry might be restructured in order for society to gain fully from its educative, socially instructive and psychologically beneficial qualities.

Vision and theory combined: the restructuring of the theatre industry

In *Theatre Outlook*, Priestley sets out by posing the questions 'What is happening to our theatre now?' and 'What ought to happen to it in the near future?' (Priestley 1947b: 14). In answering the second question he cites theatre, as 'a creative action in progress', a 'corporate affair of individual perceptions and co-operative effort' (Priestley 1947b: 52), and suggests that the theatre should be a place where 'serious professional men and women, properly trained and well-equipped, go to work as surgeons and physicians go to work'. His radical vision was that we should begin with a 'clean, bare stage, solidly set in the community and linked with hundreds of similar sensible organisations, a stage on which something good and true and glowing can be created' (Priestley 1947b: 53). In order to achieve this Priestley wanted the theatre industry restructured as a 'kind of pyramid' with the founding of a number of national theatre companies, each of which might be readily identified with different kinds of work – one might focus on the classical repertoire, another on more experimental plays and so on. Such companies would be run by experienced professional artists – he uses Basil Dean, Michael Macowan and Tyrone Guthrie as examples of possible artistic directors. The national theatres would be run on a continental model whereby they represented the 'apex' of the pyramid. Workers from these theatres would transfer to other theatres countrywide in order to skills-share: they would be paid a good wage but not one which necessarily matched high commercial rates. For Priestley (Priestley 1947b: 54–5), restructuring in such a manner would discourage the 'speculators, parasites and shoddy impresarios' whom he felt had dominated the British theatre of the first half of the twentieth century. Instead of having these theatres managed through a pursuit of profit, they would be overseen by a 'National Theatre Authority', which to Priestley (1947b) was more preferable to the partisan and ruling class dominated Arts Council. Priestley's ideas for restructuring bear a remarkable resemblance to what has actually happened in part, through the impact of state funding, in British theatre since the 1950s.

Priestley wanted the organisation of theatre culture to be networked and this involved provision in educational institutions. He proposed what was then a radical rethink of the ways in which drama and theatre featured as part of the curriculum in higher education. He wanted universities to have their own drama departments with theatres, studios and workshops, as opposed to housing 'drama' within literature departments. A remarkably progressive vision, he urged for these departments to have a real working relationship with professional practice which they could explore through student placements and through workshops with playwrights and critics. Priestley also wanted to organise the civic theatres, suggesting that each city or larger town should have at least 'two good sized theatres', one for touring companies which might include the national theatres mentioned above, and one for the local civic companies who would model themselves to some extent on the national ones. The civic theatres would be run by public corporations funded through the municipality, the Arts Council and private donations in order that the theatre might be financed from a number of sources and so be less susceptible to the political contrivances of municipal governance (Priestley 1947b: 59). These civic theatres should be seen as part of a package of public amenities and should have no less status than public parks, galleries and libraries. Priestley believed they would develop and reflect local identities and civic pride.

For smaller geographical settings – towns and villages – Priestley suggested a 'Group System' theatre whereby the communities shared amenities and organised themselves and their theatres, many of which had fallen into disrepair before and after the Second World War. He proposed that such communities could arrange transport and tours between towns and so share the costs of rehearsal and production, capitalising as much as possible on theatre companies already functioning well in the area. As part of this plan, Priestley felt that the professional and amateur theatre might mutually benefit each other with the sharing of performance spaces and skills.

Theory: the state and the theatre

Priestley's pyramid structure intentionally removed British theatre from the commercial economic model. In this he shared in common ideas which Shaw, William Archer and Granville Barker had proposed before him. But Priestley took their ideas a step further in that his metropolitan model showed clear pathways for influencing theatre country-wide and not just in London. Just as Matthew Arnold had demanded that the English should 'organise the theatre' in the late 1870s (see Stokes 1972: 3–9), so Priestley created an imaginary multilayered, interconnected national, realisable restructuring and organisation for British theatre, based in part on a projected ideal and in part on using what already existed. Arnold and Priestley shared in common a belief in state subsidy and although Priestley was aware of the many pitfalls of such a system of financial backing, he insisted that the state should take responsibility.

> Among the enemies of the Theatre we must still include the British Government, which, with the hearty approval of all parties does not care whether the Theatre lives or dies as long as it pays the ferocious tax imposed upon it. . . .
>
> The State is really the greatest shareholder in all our theatrical enterprises, and a shareholder who invests nothing, takes no interest in what is being created, but yet contrives to grab between a third and a quarter of all the takings at the box office. Even when everybody else concerned is losing money, the Treasury is still taking its fat cut.
>
> . . . If the treasury actually took nothing from the Theatre, it would still owe the Theatre something, because of the millions it receives in Entertainment Duty from the films . . . theatre seats, like books, are comparatively the cheapest luxury things we can buy nowadays . . . a far greater pro-portion of the millions collected should be returned to the

Theatre, in the form of generous subsidies to non-commercial companies with a very high standard of work.

(Priestley 1947b: 22–6)

In *The Arts under Socialism* (1947) written after the Labour landslide of 1945, Priestley suggested that a socialist society could provide a better context for the provision of arts, claiming that, 'the creation of and appreciation of the arts . . . is one of the ends towards which the socialist state is the means' (Priestley 1947c: 5–6). Art should not be treated as the 'icing on the cake' of social planning and policy, rather, provision of support should be central. The state should encourage good publishing houses, book shops, and provide concert halls, opera houses and theatres as a sign of its appreciation of the importance of art. Priestley wanted the state to support arts' unions and protect its artists from exploitation by strengthening, for example, copyright laws. He wanted the state to set up committees which would enable rather than inhibit: his feeling about the newly formed Arts Council at this point, was that it was run by officials and 'busybodies' who knew nothing about the theatre and cared very little for it.

Theatre critics of the era, such as James Agate, believed that they should not get involved in 'theatre politics' and by implication, that Priestley should be wary of doing so. They rarely shared his utopian vision of the arts under socialism, as Agate's attitude exemplifies:

there won't be any art under socialism. The only books, music and pictures that have ever been worth a damn were written, composed, painted at a time when the Czars . . . and the upper classes whipped the lower classes for the entertainment of their guests after dinner. I do not want books, plays and symphonic poems written around communal wash-houses.[5]

Priestley was well informed about the provision of arts in communist countries (see Priestley 1946) and understood the pitfalls of 'committee' art and the types of state intervention which had the potential to censor rather than encourage creativity. Nevertheless, he believed that a socialist state could differentiate from a capitalist one in refusing to be 'terrified of the passion and insight, the vast generosity and searching vision of the great artists' (Priestley 1947c: 6). Art could reflect upon and build the spirit of a generation, and in the context of post Second World War Britain, this was a process which Priestley saw as requiring state support and facilitation. Just as he had suggested state support for the financial and organisational restructuring of the theatre industry, so he urged for the state to support the arts as a fundamental component of its future social planning. This links Priestley directly to the progressive thinkers of his age – those who created the community oriented Welfare State (see Addison 1977).

Theory and practice: the playwright as interventionist – J.B. Priestley as theatre producer

> I enjoyed working in the Theatre but never saw it, as so many people did then, as a glittering playground . . . I disliked the West End Theatre in its glamour-gossip-column aspect. Though often successful, I was never a fashionable play-wright. So far as I appealed to any particular class, I would say this was the professional middle class. (This possibly explains why I was so widely and often produced abroad, where Theatre-going tended to be more serious – not so much a party-night-out affair as it was in the West End).
>
> (*Guardian*, 5 April 1974, quoted in Priestley 2005: 28)

Priestley strongly believed in the right, and at times the necessity, for the playwright to act as interventionist. Perhaps because of this, his was a 'love/hate' relationship with the British theatre establishment during the 1930s, 1940s and 1950s. Neither his political leanings nor his aesthetic beliefs were in tune with those – politically more conservative – who had managerial control of what was, or was not, produced in the commercial sector of the British theatre industry. This is not to say that other play-wrights of his generation did not also suffer under such a system: productions with 'star' casts or productions of plays by play-wrights with a track record of attracting consistent audiences were favoured. Within this system of cultural production, a playwright was only ever as good as their last play. Priestley often had more than one play running in the West End, thus actually benefited from a system which he condemned. However, from early on Priestley took control of the production of the vast majority of his work, by founding his own production company; it was also through this company that a number of plays by other 'new' playwrights were premiered. Priestley's foray into independent management began with his association with J.P. Mitchelhill, who by the early 1930s owned the Duchess Theatre and produced plays, a number of which become classics such as the controversial *Children in Uniform* (1932, by Christa Winslow), Emlyn Williams' *Night Must Fall* (1935) and T.S. Eliot's *Murder in the Cathedral* (1936). It was under Mitchelhill's management of the Duchess that Priestley's *Laburnum Grove* (1933), *Eden End* (1934), *Cornelius* (1935), *Spring Tide* (1936) and *Time and the Conways* (1937) were produced. According to director Michael Macowan, Priestley was brought in as producer/backer to their production company, the London Mask Theatre Company, which had operated out of the privately owned Westminster Theatre, after the 1937 season,

> I can't remember the figures now, it may have been two thousand five hundred or five thousand . . . he said he'd put up half and we'd find somebody to put up the other half.
>
> (Cotes 1977: 48)

Priestley's financing of the London Mask Theatre Company (see Cotes 1977) was interrupted by the war, but after this point, Mitchelhill became the chair of the company which now included Thane Parker, Ronald Jeans, Michael Macowan and Priestley. *The Linden Tree* (1947) was their first major post-war success, and the company went on to produce Priestley's *Eden End* (in revival, in 1948), *Home is Tomorrow* (1948) and *Summer Day's Dream* (1949).

Priestley had initially gone into production in order to escape what he saw as 'the worst effects' of the dominant production system in London as outlined earlier in this chapter. He enjoyed 'working on the production side with friends like directors Irene Hentschel and Basil Dean and Michael Macowan, and on the managerial side with other colleagues like his agent A.D. Peters, J.P. Mitchelhill and Thane Parker' (Priestley 1962: 197). It should also be pointed out that as a shrewd businessman, he made money from this venture: his percentage of production profits could be added to the normal author's fee. Thus his standard share of gross weekly box office takings for *The Linden Tree* was 10 per cent or 7.5 per cent if takings were less than £1000 and 5 per cent if they were under £800. His royalties were limited to £5000, with any owing after this to be reinvested in the London Mask Theatre Company.[6]

On other productions, while one-third of the profits would go to the theatre, two-thirds might go to Priestley as the 'backer'. Thus, with a production such as *Laburnum Grove* (1933), running costs were relatively low at about £620 per week, while takings, over the production run, remained fairly constant. At an average profit of around £250 plus per week (worth around £11,575 in today's currency minus the 33.3 per cent Entertainments Tax levy), Priestley stood to make a substantial amount in addition to the offer of $5000 by Paramount [film] Productions for a film treatment or adaptation in 1936.[7] A good businessman, Priestley was exceptional in his willingness to actively reinvest money in theatre.

In his 1962 autobiography *Margin Released*, which contains the most about his theatre work, he pointed to the fact that G.B. Shaw 'did not approve' of his production company which, it should be stressed, produced plays by other writers as well as his own.

> At the time Shaw was declaring that any manager who revived his plays at cheap prices would make a fortune. He had only to make a telephone call or two and then find his cheque-book to begin testing the truth of this assertion, but he never did. He told me . . . that management would ruin me; it was a short cut to bankruptcy. He was quite wrong.
>
> (Priestley 1962: 198)

Priestley's business sense revealed a real understanding of the complexities of the economics of production and of the desirability of artistic control. Just as his initial collaboration with Mitchelhill had helped to solidify his reputation as a playwright (see Cotes 1977), so too had this venture enabled him to prove his theory that the playwright did not have to be a passive participant in the processes of production.

> This was in the Thirties, when we could produce *Laburnum Grove*, or *Eden End* or *Time and The Conways* for about £800, and the weekly running costs – the 'get out' or 'nut' were around the same figure, theatre and all. The profits . . . were never gigantic . . . I was never a showman . . . I prefer the legitimate stage to be quiet, solid, bourgeois. That Great Theatre . . . would be . . . an author's theatre.
>
> (Priestley 1962: 198)

Priestley's time of hands-on production management ended around the end of the 1940s, but his business acumen continued. Here, we have to remember that Priestley's plays have continued to be produced all over the world, with often more than one production of any one play running at any one time; the example of eight productions of *Eden End* running in professional and amateur theatres in England during September of 1972 is a case in point.[8] Priestley engaged with playwriting as a profession in an active manner, from a creative, practical and business point of view.

Practice: the playwright

> There is . . . a bad tradition in the commercial English-speaking Theatre . . . the author is some poor little chap, creeping in and out of rehearsals, waiting to be noticed, who has put together a lot of stuff that the management, the producer, the players, out of their experience and superior knowledge, might be able to shape into something like a play
> . . .

The Theatre that handles him in this fashion cannot be taken seriously in any account of dramatic art: it is in the entertainment industry and nothing more.

(Priestley 1957: 53–4)

Priestley had much to offer in the way of an analysis of the craft of playwriting. His writings on theatre history and dramatic literature expose a sophisticated transhistorical knowledge of the work of both European playwrights and theories of playwriting. As was the case with other forms of writing, Priestley took a very practical approach to both his critiques of their work and to the ensuing advice he gave to would-be playwrights. He insisted that playwrights had an artistic duty not to pander to the tastes of commercial production managements.

> Bring life into Theatre, the Theatre into life. Think in terms of action, for though plays are mostly dialogue, the talk should be moving towards an action. . . . Assume that the drama of debate is Shaw's copyright, so don't have people sitting around discussing the atom bomb, unless one of them has an atom bomb and proposes to use it. Try to have a continuous and varied series of little dramas within your big drama; the ability to write like this marks the born dramatist . . . Brecht . . . wanted to remove the drama from private life, give it an historical sweep, make it suggest the fate of whole classes . . . which sacrifices nearly everything I want in a playhouse. If I were beginning again I would move in the opposite direction, towards more elaborate construction and even greater intimacy, taking a few characters through an intricate and ironic dance of relationships.
>
> (Priestley 1957: 29–30)

Priestley clearly believed in a 'playwright's theatre', but for him the playwright was part of a creative community, part of a team. He saw the contemporary management of theatre production as working against the creativity of playwriting; the playwright was supposed to write the play and then submit it for production, and it was often the case that the relationship between the playwright and the production of their play ended at this point. His encouragement of playwrights to take an active role in the process of production was underpinned by his belief that this was one way of subverting a situation whereby

> the success or failure of theatrical production is largely determined by chance and accident ... in the English-speaking Theatre you are compelled to exist in an over-heated atmosphere of dazzling successes and shameful flops, you are a wonder man in October, a pretentious clown in March, you are in, you are out. ... You feel you have one foot in the playhouse and the other in the stock exchange. ... All this has nothing to do with the dramatic art; it is not even sensible business.
>
> (Priestley 1962: 196–7)

Although Priestley engaged with this 'business', he genuinely did so in order to create real opportunities for other writers to have their work produced in a setting they were unlikely to experience in the commercialised sectors of the industry. He wanted playwrights to be allowed 'to experiment, to take a chance. After all it is not easy to write a good play. The Theatre as a vital modern institution cannot exist without a supply of good new plays' (*New York Times*, 16 December 1934, quoted in Priestley 2005: 27)

Practice: the critics and critical reception

Mid-twentieth century theatre critics – usually men and often educated at Oxford or Cambridge – held sway over the theatre during the period in which Priestley was actively playwriting. There was very little movement between employers and so critics usually worked for the same newspaper over a substantial number of years. Some, such as Charles Morgan, H. Chance Newton and St John Ervine, either had also been actors or were playwrights themselves, but the majority, certainly by the 1950s, considered themselves to be full-time critics, attending the openings of new productions and sometimes reviewing transfers of successful ones. As the period progressed, critics moved more towards a form of criticism which fed into celebritised culture, commenting on gossip and the fashionable. Walter Macqueen-Pope, theatre publicist, manager and self-styled theatre historian whose professional life spanned more than fifty years, felt that as the century moved on, audiences became more concerned with 'celebrity' spotting and the press critics played into this (Macqueen-Pope 1959: 33–6). Although an overgeneralised analysis, it contains a strong element of truth. The theatre provided an opportunity to participate in a culture of display, which often had little to do with 'art' and more to do with 'fashion' and the fashionable. That audiences became somehow less sophisticated in their tastes is questioned by others (see Bason 1931), but the circulation of celebrity gossip and the appeal of theatre as a place of glamour, where 'stars' could be seen in the flesh as opposed to in celluloid only, was seen by Priestley to have had a negative impact both on theatre – which should be based on ensemble playing – and playwriting as a profession. His feeling was that critics should not pander to this culture but should take the art of criticism more seriously.

> Without knowing what they are doing, quite a number of our dramatic critics are busy hindering and not helping the serious Theatre. I respect the dramatic critic who writes about a play as if it were a private performance for himself, who never mentions box offices, who sees the thing purely as a work of art and not as a social event and a financial enterprise. Many critics assume that their readers are half-witted. They are careful to warn them off any play that has a glimmer of intelligence about it. The result is they are no longer on the side of serious Theatre. . . . It is a pity that critics are for ever condemned to visit theatres on first nights and on no other nights. If they did . . . they would come to understand the differences between audiences who had been bamboozled in by showmanship and publicity . . . and audiences who were really and actively playgoing, eager, excited. . . . Theatre is

battling against horribly heavy odds. . . . Keep right out, or join in Mr Critic, but do not interfere on the wrong side.

(Spectator, 19 April 1935,
quoted in Priestley 2005: 125–6)

As far as Priestley was concerned, the 'opinion of any fairly intelligent actor or actress is far sounder than that of most of these [university] learned critics' (Priestley 1957: 67). Other critics, whose influence on box office takings was discernible, were felt by Priestley to lack any willingness to engage with a need to, 'raise the standard of production and acting'. For Priestley this involved reviewing plays as theatre *not* as literature, and in terms of 'Social Content, Experiment, and Higher Standard'. He noted that a 'few of the older critics, not unappreciative of both Social Content and Higher Standard, always fall down on Experiment . . . they forget that the naturalistic play that they admire was itself once an experiment, the challenge of an advanced Theatre' (*Theatre Newsletter*, December 1948, quoted in Priestley 2005: 127–8). Priestley was not constantly in combat with critics; some, such as Ivor Brown and James Agate, were counted among his friends. But he clearly believed that they had a duty to the theatre as an art form which went beyond the partisan remit of their particular employers, he wanted sound objective criticism within a framework in which he knew that 'dramatic criticism . . . does not base its judgements on any generally accepted critical standards' (Priestley 1957: 18–19).

Often criticised for being 'populist' at the same time as being criticised for being too obscure, some critics did not like Priestley's more socially conscious plays like *They Came to a City* (1943), wondering why he did not stick to the successful comic formula of *Laburnum Grove* (1933) or *When We Are Married* (1938), plays which reveal a 'northern' humour for which Priestley was famous. Agate notes Priestley's belief that a playwright 'should not be content to fill old forms with new matter but discover or invent new forms' (Agate 1948: 166) but disliked his more experimental work such as *They Came to a City* (1943), feeling that it appealed only to 'young people devoid of dramatic perception', or *Johnson Over Jordan* (1939) which he felt to be experimental in form but not content (Agate 1946: 78–9). Priestley condemned Agate and his colleagues for doing little to change the theatre industry, pointing out that when he and Ronald Jeans subsidised the Westminster Theatre just before the Second World War, 'just to give London some intelligent productions at easy prices', Agate's attitude was 'grudging and querulous'. Agate and his colleagues played into a theatre system whereby a successful play might be given only a few days 'get-out' notice because the theatre owners had something on 'standby' out of which they thought they could make more money (Priestley 1947a: 185–6). Priestley wanted critics to help improve working and production conditions for playwrights, not spend their time criticising those like himself for 'magnificent sermonising' or writing 'sociologically' (Agate 1946: 78–9).

That Priestley engaged so actively and at times formidably with the critics was unusual for a playwright of his generation: one might suggest that he took up the cause where G.B. Shaw left off. To an extent he could do this because his success had given him financial stability, but this success had only come about as a result of the fact that he was able to tune in to what it was that potential audiences were looking for. Here, *They Came to a City*, which ran for eight months, is a good case in point. Produced during the Second World War, and questioning the relationship of class and community to modes of living, it presented a discussion of utopian social visions for a wartime audience hungry for some recognition of the hardship of their recent experiences. Priestley did not see himself as writing plays with a 'message'; as he reminds us, 'it would never occur to me to wrap up a message in a hundred pages of a play script' as this is not the 'business of theatre' (*Theatre Newsletter*, 1948, quoted in Priestley 2005: 128). Although his plays can be grouped in terms of their focus on particular social, political or philosophical issues, the groupings do not necessarily represent 'phases' in his playwriting.

Thus, from the mid to late 1930s his processing of theories of time are played out in *Time and the Conways* (1937) and *I Have Been Here Before* (1937) but these reverberate in plays from the 1940s as well. Similarly the critique of capitalism, present in a comedy like *Bees on the Boat Deck* (1936) and *Cornelius* (1940), is also prevalent in *An Inspector Calls* (1946), *Home is Tomorrow* (1948) and *Summer Day's Dream* (1949). Priestley did not see himself as a 'political' playwright but political thinking drives his playwriting: equally, his ability to write comic drama lies at the heart of many of his plays. In light of this, his 'criticism of the critics', as it were, was shaped by his belief that a playwright's oeuvre should be allowed to express an ever changing commitment to an art form. By contrast he saw most critics as operating in favour of a theatre system which inhibited playwrights from developing their work, because it relied on the marketing of products: if one management found success with a certain type of play, another management would want to ape that success by seeking to produce a play which it understood to capitalise on a similar formula. Priestley wanted a 'serious' theatre which allowed for intelligent audiences and intelligent but entertaining plays. That he found such continual success over an initial period of more than thirty years, despite the 'nightmare obstacle course' that the theatre industry represented, implies that his vision of what theatre culture might be, has been shared by audiences of a number of generations, both in Europe and North America.

Part II
Key plays

3 The family, gender and sexual relations

A number of critics have tried to frame Priestley's playwriting into phases based either on chronology (pre-war, wartime and post-war) or on areas of thematic focus – time, socialism and the post-war world (Klein 1988: 245). It could be argued that such divisions are effectively irrelevant as Priestley returned to themes at different points in his playwriting career, and equally, aspects of socialist thinking have a sustained centrality in his work. One might see his playwriting as developing in line with his growing involvement in the processes of making theatre: the more he was involved in production and management the more aesthetic demands he made on the medium. The staging of plays from the early 1930s is far less complex than those from the late 1930s and early 1940s such as *Johnson Over Jordan* (see Chapter 8) and *They Came to a City* (1943) for example (see Chapter 5). However we choose to frame his plays, DeVitis and Kalson (1980) rightly point out that while Priestley became the 'disillusioned optimist' as he matured, he never lost sight of a Jungian emphasis on man's goodness and the 'concept of the oneness of all men'. This oneness places man as 'a member of a charmed or magic circle': at the centre of the circle is the family and as his career progresses Priestley widens the circle to embrace the 'nation as family' and the 'world as family' (DeVitis and Kalson 1980: 125). Such an analysis to some extent oversimplifies Priestley's reading and appropriation of Jung, but it does provide an interesting framework which pinpoints the importance of the concept and actuality of the family as a social and socialising unit in his plays.

The idea of the family, as a domestic and social unit, both nuclear/extended and biological/sociological, lies at the heart of a great number of Priestley's plays. He is not atypical in this: many other playwrights of the 1930s and 1940s used representations and analyses of the family and changing gender roles within it, as a way of reflecting on social and political events and transitions – this is particularly so in the case of the numerous women playwrights of the era in which Priestley was working in the theatre (see Gale 1996, 2000) but is also the case for a number of male playwrights traditionally viewed as conservative, such as Somerset Maugham and Noël Coward. Historically, the family as a social unit had undergone a significant transformation during the first fifty years of the twentieth century, not only because of the two world wars in which whole generations of men had died, but also because of increases in social mobility and leisure time and a significant increase in the levels of professionalisation among lower-middle and middle-class women. With two world wars only some twenty-one years apart, two out of three generations of women had differentiated expectations in terms of their place in the employment market. Women were often required to work in traditionally 'male' vocations during each of the two world wars and, although legislation and social theory aimed to reverse the position after each, by the 1950s middle-class women were a strong component of the workforce. With the newly acquired partial franchise in 1918 and the full vote in 1928, women had growing social power as voting citizens, despite the various Married Women's Laws which prohibited them working in certain professions once married (see Lewis 1984).

Such transformations were bound to change the structure and operation of the family as a working unit, and this was something of which Priestley was aware. In an essay published in the early 1920s, 'In Praise of the Normal Woman', he berated the generation of 'elderly men' who were 'secretly terrified' by the 'new type of woman':

> the emancipated woman, who has put down her fancy-work, left home, received a man's education, taken a man's position in the world, and partly adopted masculine habits.
>
> (Priestley 1967b: 85)

Priestley himself, in a strange twist of logic, did not fear such women because, for him, they operated on the same basis as men and so did not have the power to question or criticise 'male' behaviour – they were masculinised. He suggested that the 'ordinary woman'

> usually possesses something that her more 'advanced' sister plainly lacks, and that is common sense; and a measure of feminine commonsense is fatal to pretentious and designing males. . . . As for the free-and-easy banter of the mannish women, their pontifical airs, their pedantry, their shrill sarcasms, they are simply ineffectual, a mere play of shadows, compared with this older method of feminine attack and defence, the method of polite smiling irony.
>
> (Priestley 1967b: 87)

Underpinning his somewhat perverse analysis is a belief that the imitation of power structures does not undermine the power structures themselves. In other words, if women behave in a way which is culturally recognised as masculine, then such masculine behaviour is being ratified rather than questioned. Priestley strongly believed that the feminine and the masculine were oppositions, the dynamics and manifestations of which could be easily formulated. His own early oversimplified divisions of gendered behaviour are not borne out in his plays where the feminine and the masculine are made more complex and interwoven. Indeed women feature as the heroines or the narrative drivers of many of his plays. Moreover, it is important to remember that his division of the sexes, unlike many others who critiqued the emancipation of women, was not based on the idea that either the feminine or the masculine was superior to the other. Placed in cultural context, there were a number of feminists who believed that the emancipation of women should include access to and control of the power structures, but that this should not necessitate the removal, rather the integration, of the 'feminine' in such systems of power. The cultural anxiety around the idea of a 'petticoat government' after women were given the full franchise was virulent, and Priestley's early essay tries to identify some of the elements of this anxiety without actually acknowledging that it is doing so. His simple unravelling of a complex social issue may seem old fashioned to a contemporary audience nowadays, but it was radical in its time because of his underlying belief that the sexes were 'different but equal': such an analysis reverberates in the arguments around women's emancipation during the second wave of feminism in the 1970s and 1980s.

It is important to unpick some of Priestley's early ideas on gender, because questions around gender are central to many of his 'family' plays and gendered behaviour as a social construct is an issue to which he returns on numerous occasions. Similarly, his understanding of gender and the way in which it operates is also integral to his dramatic representations of the family, where often women are both central and represent two extremes of the ideological spectrum. Priestley was fascinated by women on a personal level, and his own experiences of family life were complex. His mother died when he was young, his first wife died when he was in his early thirties, his second wife spent the war years setting up and managing homes for evacuated children,[1] and he had five children of his own and two through marriages to divorced women. Often presented as a womaniser (see Brome 1988), Priestley's autobiographical writing pays witness to the importance which the family, as a supportive domestic unit, held in his professional as well as personal life. Interestingly however, his dramatic depictions of the traditional family unit are often of a social structure in collapse, the foundations disturbed by social and political events, the cosy traditions remodelled through necessity. While his first play, the adaptation of *The Good Companions* (see Chapter 6), creates a 'virtual' family – the performance troupe function as an extended family unit but one which has chosen its members – the second *Dangerous Corner* (1932) unpicks comfortable middle-class complacency and shows the traditional family as both dysfunctional and in crisis.

The family in a state of disintegration from *Dangerous Corner* (1932) to *The Glass Cage* (1957)

Dangerous Corner (1932)

Dangerous Corner has become one of Priestley's most performed plays, although as with a number of his works, it was not well received by the critics on original production. A revised text, which missed out the radio device at the beginning of the play and reformulated some of the language to suit an American audience, premiered in New York five months after the London production and ran for over 1000 performances. Thus, while his most successful play on Broadway during this period, the London production ran for just 150 performances at the Lyric in London in 1932. Since this point, however, it has become, with the obvious exception of *An Inspector Calls*, one of his most popular plays; similar to *An Inspector Calls*, its immediate popularity was outside of England (see Chapter 7). Pre-publicity for the London production framed it as 'a study in a satirical vein of the post-War generation',[2] while the critics who responded positively to the production framed it more specifically in terms of Priestley's critique of the 'tedious, teasing suburbanity' of the Caplan family at the centre of the play.[3] One reviewer recognised the way in which Priestley had taken the then current 'drawing room', middle-class family play and turned it upside down.

> Mr Priestley has looked upon the theatrical drawing-room and has been, with good reason, a little bored by it. The stuff of drama, he says by implication, is in men's hands; there is always, beneath their reticences, a clash of their secret knowledge and suspicions, of their hatreds and loves of one another, and this clash, existing though none perceives it, is no less dramatic because, in life it is repressed and finds no outlet in action. His aim is to make this clash audible, to discover a drawing-room's soul.[4]

Figure 2 Dangerous Corner, Lyric Theatre, London, 1932.

The play sees Priestley manipulating the detective format and using a time device to confuse the audience (see Chapter 4). The plot is seemingly uncomplex. The Caplan family women and their guest, Miss Mockridge – a popular novelist whose novels are published by the Caplan family publishing house – are listening to the radio in the drawing room. Discussion ensues about the radio play which has just finished, when the family men and their guest come to join the women. Conversation then begins to focus on a cigarette box which Olwen Peel, an honorary family member who has worked for the family firm for some years, claims to have seen before. Freda Caplan, wife of Robert – now the family patriarch – suggests that Olwen can't have seen the box before as it was a gift from her to the diseased Martin Caplan – Robert's brother – given to him on the day he committed suicide. Olwen then tries to cover her tracks and end the discussion, but Robert pushes her and the focus then moves to an awkward and heated discussion about Martin and the events leading up to his death.

As the play progresses through its three acts, we discover that each of the family members have had significant dealings with Martin of which the others are unaware. Thus, the family outsiders Olwen, Stanton and Miss Mockridge, each in their own way, contribute to an uncomfortable unpicking of the threads which have held the family together. Freda Caplan had been having an affair with Martin; her brother Gordon had also, it is implied, been in love with Martin, who had exploited his affections; Robert, Freda's husband and Martin's brother, had been in love with Betty, Gordon's wife; she in turn had been having an illicit affair with Stanton, whose affiliations with the family business had been substantial and long-lived; finally Olwen, desperately in love with Robert, had been the object of Stanton's secret affections. This all sounds somewhat farcical and is a deliberate play on a romantic comedy format, yet all of the relationships or romantic longings are deeply problematic and ultimately unhappy ones. Equally, each of the unravellings of emotional truths are linked to the characters' relationship to Martin, who as the 'attractive and quixotic' brother is drawn in stark contrast to the upright and 'proper' Robert (Hughes 1958: 131).

Martin is assumed to have stolen money from the family firm and this, it is believed, is the reason behind his decision to take his own life. What is revealed, as an echo of Freud, is that Martin's id rather than his ego or super ego, was ruling his life and that unlike his brother, he did not repress his sexuality nor did he try to quash his own drug addiction. Happy to be in receipt of the devotion of both his brother's wife and her own brother, Martin felt far from guilty about any of his selfish actions. Stanton in actuality stole the money and when this fact was not discovered during the court inquest after Martin's death, he was content to keep quiet about it. Gordon, devoted to Martin's Apollonian nature, was one of the key witnesses at the hearing while others in the family absented themselves. As the play draws to a close and each has taken the 'dangerous corner' and revealed their own 'truth' – their moral complicity in Martin's death – Olwen speaks up and turns out to be the last of all of them to have seen Martin alive.

OLWEN: . . . He saw himself as some sort of Pan. . . . He thought of me . . . as a priggish spinster . . . and kept telling me that my dislike of him showed that I was trying to repress a great fascination he had for me . . . I'd never lived, never would live . . . I was sorry for him, because really he was ill, sick in mind and body, and I thought perhaps I could calm him down. . . . He was one of our own set, mixed up with most of the people I liked best in the world . . . he was in that excited abnormal state . . . then he tried to show me some beastly foul drawing he has – horrible obscene things . . . then he was telling me to take my clothes off . . . he stood between me and the door.

(Priestley 2001a: 78–9)

Martin's attempted rape of Olwen failed because the revolver he was wielding got turned against him in the struggle, and went off by mistake. When the family find out what happened, they do not turn on Olwen but sympathise with her. It is Stanton who receives their wrath because of his theft of family money and his theft and exploitation of Betty's affections. Robert, who has forced out the truth, now finds he has lost the comfort of illusion: when told by Olwen that he will have to learn to live without illusions, he replies:

ROBERT: . . . Can't be done. Not for us. We started life too early for that, possibly now they are breeding people who can live without illusions. . . . But I can't do it. I've lived among illusions. . . . They've given me hope and courage . . . I suppose we ought to get all that from faith in life. But I haven't got any. No religion or anything. . . . But it didn't look too bad. I'd my little illusions . . . we are not living in the same *world* now. Everything's gone.

(Priestley 2001a: 92)

As the family clash and blame one another, Robert disappears, the stage goes to blackout and a shot is heard. When the lights come up the scene is the same as at the beginning of the play and the women are listening to the radio: the dialogue then runs to almost exactly the same pattern as during the opening of Act I until the mention of the cigarette box, but nobody questions Olwen about having seen it before and the lights fade as they all carry on chatting and listening to the same play, aptly named, as at the opening of Act I, *The Sleeping Dog*, on the radio.

In twisting the end of the play so that we return in a loop to the beginning, Priestley recreates the closed circularity which the family have broken through during the play, as we have witnessed it. He employs a theatrical device through which we now see the Caplans and their associates in a different light, although we are not sure that anything we have witnessed has 'really' happened – were we just watching a staging of a radio play? Were we just seeing the working out of a plot as conceived in the mind of the novelist Miss Mockridge? Such possibilities are unlikely, but Priestley clearly dislocates our trust in the realism of that which we have just observed. Robert has instigated the deconstruction of the family, like the peeling of an onion, and at its centre lies the 'corrupted' Martin, Robert's alter ego, a man who refused to confine himself to the repressive qualities of middle-class family values and traditions. Miss Mockridge's 'charmed circle', as she describes the group at the beginning of the play, is broken, the 'snug little group' has been disbanded. Not even Priestley's switch back to the pre-confessional moments of the play can reverse the fact that the foundations on which the family had built its identity, have been severely undermined. And this is of course a deliberate strategy on his part, we are invited to believe in the integrity of the middle-class family unit and then witness the unpicking of all the threads which have held it together.

Martin Caplan, who never appears and whose character is entirely constructed through the descriptions of those around him, is the central force in the play; he is the family member who has lived outside the traditional mores which the family has established. It is surprising that his bisexuality and drug addiction are so overt, given the censorship laws which prevailed over theatres and playwrights at the time (see Nicholson 2003). The fact of his lack of physical presence in the play may have dampened the censor's desire to ban the play: the censor's report suggests that

Martin's bisexuality was not considered to be 'threatening'. The reader's report for the censor's office states that there was 'nothing in the revelations to trouble us', that the play contained 'the suggestion of sentimental homosexuality' which was 'only vague and non-physical'.[5] For Alan Sinfield (1999: 170), Martin represents the infiltration 'by queerness' of a bourgeois family group, yet it might be said that Priestley is offering us more than this. Rather than presenting homosexuality in the negative, Martin is bisexual, his sexuality is not contained by gendered preference and functions outside of either heterosexuality or homosexuality: he is an individualist uninterested in continuing family traditions and his presence demands that we review the nature of inclusivity and exclusivity within the family unit.

A number of reviews of the play mention the fact that Priestley sets out to demolish 'the houses of illusion' which the Caplans and the bourgeois family unit they represent live within.[6] Equally they criticise his desire to probe into family politics – 'a husband who insists on uncovering the cesspool would have desisted at the first hint of a bad smell'[7] – and allow the ghosts of the past to haunt, but this is clearly deliberate on Priestley's part. Many of the critics also bemoaned the fact that the characters were not 'likeable', and that this somehow undermined the power of the play. But just as more recent productions, such as Laurie Sansom's for the West Yorkshire Playhouse/Garrick Theatre in 2001, present the Caplans and their associates as a 'snug little group' of 'beautiful young people', so Priestley was trying to delve beneath the surface of the seemingly untouchable upper-middle-class family unit of the 1930s (see Laurie Sansom in Priestley 2001: 12).

The Glass Cage (1957)

Religious bigotry, financial greed and exclusivity lie at the root of the undoing of the McBane family in Priestley's late play *The Glass Cage* (1957), which originally ran for a short period at the Piccadilly Theatre in London's West End.[8] The setting is Canada, during the Edwardian era in 1906. Far removed from the 1950s in which it was written, Priestley turns back the clock as a means of looking at issues around heritage, religion and exclusion using the family unit and the disintegration of the foundations which serve as its basis as a central focal point for dramatic action. Writing in the context of the emergence of a post-colonial, post-nuclear and post-war Britain, the play is an extraordinarily modern piece steeped in philosophical questioning and displays a virile ability on Priestley's part to deconstruct the dynamics of religious hypocrisy, generational and cultural difference. The young people in the play, both those from the inner circle of the McBane family and those who represent the excluded outsiders – Jean, Douglas and Angus, the children of the outlawed Charlie McBane – have a contemporary demeanour. They come across as the new generation of the 1950s not of the Edwardian era.

The McBanes are an extended family: David McBane, a preacher and businessman, is the family patriarch. His wife has died and he and his daughter Elspie share a home with Mildred McBane. Along with his brother Malcolm and sister-in-law, Mildred, David heads the family business established at the latter end of the nineteenth century. His religious fervour is Presbyterian in nature and his nephew Harvey, much to his joy, is also training to be a preacher. David's religious leanings are used to justify his hardline politics on clean living and godly thinking and behaviour: he is the head of a business empire and the head of a family unit which lies at the centre of the community in which he resides. The family are awaiting the arrival of the three children of his dead and once wayward brother Charlie. Their presence has been requested in order that they may sign off on some papers relating to the ownership of the family business. At the same time as presenting the three in terms of their relationship to the family, David is also clear that they are outsiders and do not share the beliefs or privileges of his own immediate family. Their father was an alcoholic who had more in common with the loggers and working men who were his own employees. Equally, David is clear that the fact that their mother was 'a wild girl' from 'Thunder Bay country – part Indian' (that is to say, Native American) locates them as 'other', as outsiders (Priestley 2003b: 200). Yet as Dr Gratton, an old friend of the family reminds them, in terms of heritage Charlie actually provided the most children for the family line. As he says, 'David a widower, with only little Elspie here.

And Robert McBane left you a childless widow, Mildred. And Malcolm here is not even married' (Priestley 2003b: 200). While Mildred claims that David went to a great deal of trouble to find Charlie's children, who were dispersed all over the country, she is also unwilling to be a welcoming hostess during their stay. She simply does not want them inside the family home. The position of overt hostility is amplified early on by Elspie, who again strongly positions them as 'other' to her everyday experience of the family. When asked what she thinks about Jean and her brothers, having just met them, she responds:

> What I felt – and it upset me, gave me the queerest shaky sort of feeling – was that they were so strange. *Really* strange, not just people I don't know. There weren't any thoughts or feelings I could understand behind their eyes . . . All three have the same sort of eyes – they just look at you.
> (Priestley 2003b: 206–7)

David McBane is keen to point out that the three outsiders *are* different but that they should be treated with kindness and respect. This is ironic in terms of what he has brought them into the family to achieve. It turns out that their father was knowingly cheated out of his share of the family business by Mildred and Malcolm, who made sure that when Charlie signed away his share in the family business, he was too inebriated to know what he was doing. Douglas McBane, the oldest of Charlie's children, undermines David's assumption that all three of his brother's offspring are stupid as well as 'heathen', and does his own detailed research into the workings of the family history and the legality of the business and its ownership. The discovery that he and his family have built their community and business profile through dishonesty shocks David and, as the play draws to a close, his position as patriarch and giver of unchallengeable orders has been undermined. John Harvey and Elspie's lives have been completely changed through their interaction with the outsiders, Malcolm and Mildred's hypocrisy has been exposed, and David has transformed into a man who is unsure about his own heritage and the solidity of his belief system.

Priestley deliberately constructs the outsiders as infiltrators and, just as with *Dangerous Corner*, it is the outsiders who force the family to re-evaluate its perception of itself as a solid and unbreakable social unit. That Jean, Douglas and Angus have made a pact to avenge their father in *The Glass Cage* is resolved through their decision at the end of the play not to take money from the McBanes and not to demand any reparation for the wrongs which were meted out to their father and by association, their mother and themselves. Jean locates herself and her brothers in terms of the world in which they were raised:

> JEAN: Our mother believed you'd all got rid of our father –
> . . . because he married *her*. And of course that seemed
> as wicked and terrible to us as it did to her . . . she slaved
> to bring us up properly – but she let us grow up in a cage
> . . . we could see the world stretching before us – through
> the glass bars – but we couldn't go out to accept it.
> (Priestley 2003b: 276)

By the end of the play Jean realises that in exposing the truth she and her brothers have a choice: she suggests that they move forward and allow themselves to be released from the 'glass cage', from which they have experienced the world thus far. Each side of the family has humanised the other – David now realises that the basis on which he was operating was false and Jean and her brothers feel that their side of the family history has been exposed and accounted for. The coloniser and the representation of the colonised are somehow reconciled knowing that their worlds have changed. Priestley is clear however, that the family unit cannot function without the exposé of fault-lines in the ideology which has hitherto held it together. The embracing of forgiveness as a way forward for Jean and her brothers serves to present their future as open, and therefore 'uncaged'. Rather than being a liberal or religious conclusion it is one in which Priestley suggests that we can be released from the control of the ghost of our pasts, that there is always an alternative way forward for both the group and the individual, although racism, however implied, prevails.

Tom Priestley has suggested that *The Glass Cage* was unusual in its overt depiction of evil but that in Elspie and Jean there are echoes of the strong young women Priestley created in earlier plays (see Priestley 2003b: 11). It is certainly the case that in a number of the earlier plays the dramatic action is dependent on forthright and assertive female characters. These are often written as pairs, each of which represents one extreme of an ideological spectrum. They often also have a prodigal quality whereby their return into the family fold creates an opportunity for reassessment of the family unit.

Prodigal daughters: *Eden End* (1934), *Time and the Conways* (1937) and *The Linden Tree* (1947)

John Stokes has suggested that the figure of the prodigal, recurrent in European drama, is 'at once profoundly unfair and deeply satisfying' (Stokes 1999: 26). Certainly the figure of the prodigal son often creates disturbance within the family unit and reconciliation, forgiveness and an unravelling of the tightly bound family unit often follows his appearance. Stokes (1999: 31) points to the proliferation of prodigal daughters and especially the fact that Stella in *Eden End*[9] was viewed by Priestley as 'a prodigal daughter as well as an actress'.

Eden End (1934)

Stella's transgressive career choice as an actress serves to emphasise the significance of her withdrawal from the expectations of the traditional gender roles which her middle-class Edwardian family background would have created for her: yet Stella's escape from the family did not happen because of any radical agenda on her part. In taking us back in time to the Edwardian pre-war years, Priestley sets up an expectation of a comfortable and trouble-free, middle-class existence, and this is the life that Stella, after years of touring with second and third rate theatre companies as far afield as Australia, imagines she is returning to. But her visions of an easy and care-free home life are based on childhood memories and the fantasy of a 'happy' middle-class family. Her return to Eden End finds her father, Dr Kirby, at the end of his career and clear that he wished he had made braver choices and challenged social conventions as his daughter has done.

> You were right Stella, to cut and run when you did. . . . I wish now that I'd had the same sort of courage.
>
> (Priestley 2001b: 47)

Clearly his favourite, Kirby finds justifications for Stella having run away and neglecting to return on the death her mother six years previously. Just as he imagines that Stella has had a glowing career, so she has convinced herself that by returning home everything would be as it once was. Stella's sister Lilian, barely a teenager when Stella left, is the one who stayed at home and looked after her ailing mother, her mourning father and Geoffrey Farrant, the man whose heart was broken when Stella left. Lilian, who once had dreams of participating in traditionally masculine adventures, tells her brother, on leave from his job in Africa,

> But I used to be much more adventurous than you and much keener on exploring and wild places. . . . Do you know what I'd have rather done than anything else in the world? I'd rather have gone with Captain Scott to the South Pole.
>
> (Priestley 2001b: 33)

Lilian's aspirations to step outside of her traditional female role were undermined by her sister who, according to Lilian, ran away without thinking about the consequences and then returned when she felt her life had become a mess. Lilian's response is typical of the sibling who has had to stay at home while the prodigal goes out into the world, and because she is female, her duty to the family has involved taking over the domestic role of the 'wife'. When Stella accuses her of being small-minded and unaware of the real misery in the wider world, Lilian simply accuses her of being self-indulgent and of wallowing in emotion and sentiment. For Lilian, Stella feeds on her ability to make others emotionally dependent on her: 'And just when they had come to depend on you again, you'd run away . . . there's no responsibility in you' (Priestley 2001b: 93).

Through the battle between the two sisters Priestley raises questions about the structure and function of the family and specifically of women's roles within it. All the men are weak, naive, full of regret or simply foolish – Dr Kirby's disappointment at his life's achievements; Stella's errant husband Charles's acting career ruined by his alcoholism and battered ego; her brother's ridiculous attempts to find a sexual partner and Geoffrey Farrant's hopeless longing for Stella as he once knew her. The women, in contrast, pose philosophical questions around issues of choice, loss and duty. Gareth Lloyd Evans notes the parallel between *Eden End* and Chekhov's *The Cherry Orchard* (Evans 1964: 82), pointing to the sense of collapse and disintegration inherent in both plays. But he also feels that by returning to 1912 as a setting, the play loses impact over time: that the distance between the original audiences' relationship to the period before the First World and our own, necessitates nostalgia rather than anything more sharply political in essence. This reading, however, removes the possibility of more sophisticated analysis. When Kirby refers to the 'muddle' they are living in the 1910s and suggests that future generations in the 1930s won't understand the nature of that 'muddle', Priestley is, as Stokes suggests, nudging the audience 'towards the recognition that, in truth, "the muddle" has only deepened' (Stokes 1999: 32). But *Eden End* is more than a play about the Edwardian middle classes, just as it is a play which has resonated with audiences beyond those of the 1930s. In using the family as a focal point for examining the relationship of the individual to the group and the group to the community at large, Priestley asserts, through the return of the prodigal daughter, the fragility of those social structures which we rely on being robust.

Time and the Conways (1937)

In *Time and the Conways*, a play which is more usually grouped with Priestley's 'time' plays (see Chapter 4), the middle-class family is shown to be equally in disarray. A play in which Priestley tried to 'evoke a tender intimate atmosphere of family life', it is also one in which the texture of the family as a working unit is undermined by the very force that is meant to hold it together (Priestley 1941a: 119). The Acts II and II of *Time and the Conways* are famously reversed so that, while the play begins in the 'present' moment of 1919 just after the end of the First World War, Act II takes us forward in time to 1937, the present moment for the original audience. Act III returns us to the temporal moment at the end of Act I, where Kay, waking from sleep, puts the veracity of the action in Act II into doubt – we are never sure if what we have seen in Act II is her dream or a playing out of the 'real' future.

Because of the reversal of time however, what we witness is both a vision of the Conways' future and a time contemporary to the audience. Here the Conways have lost the financial basis which supports the family unit as Mrs Conway's snobbery and naivety have led to poor investment decisions, in an economic climate where no such mistakes could be tolerated: she has not taken the financial advice of those she considers to be her social inferiors. The family members have been called to the Conway home to discuss family finances and we learn of their fates: Carol has died, Robin, an alcoholic and unable to find himself any permanent employment, has left his wife and children to fend for themselves, and Alan, the apple of his father's eye, has, according to his mother, 'no prospects, no ambition, no self-respect' (Priestley 1994: 58). On the death of the Conway patriarch during the late 1910s, Mrs Conway, the family matriarch, took over the running of the family affairs. It is the prodigal daughters who take her to task about her poor financial management, and specifically Madge, a teacher and spinster for whom Mrs Conway has little affection or respect. Mrs Conway refused to give Madge money to buy into a partnership of a school, preferring instead to provide financial support to her errant son Robin, 'her own sort, and a great comfort' (Priestley 1994: 58). Priestley pits one generation of women against another and uses this as a filter through which we see tradition subverted by progress in terms of gender roles within the family. The two 'prodigal daughters' Kay and Madge are both professional women but they are also living in the 'real' world: Kay would like to write novels but has to work as a journalist in order to survive, and Madge's work as a teacher reflects her strong belief in the power and necessity of education. Kay's approach to the disaster which has befallen the family since Act I is equally critical but somewhat more sanguine and less aggressive than her elder sister's. Madge accuses her mother of neglect both of the family unit and of the individuals within it.

> MADGE: But it's monstrous. When I was at home – and knew about things – we were considered quite well off. There were all the shares and property father left, not simply for mother but for all of us. And now not only has it been frittered away, but we are expected to provide for mother.
>
> (Priestley 1994: 50)

Mrs Conway suggests that her daughter hasn't 'the least idea what a woman's real life is like' (Priestley 1994: 50) but Priestley is clear that the life Mrs Conway has led is one of careless privilege. Madge notes that like many others of her own generation she had aspirations and hopes after the First World War, 'When I still thought we could suddenly make everything better for everybody. Socialism! Peace! Universal Brotherhood!' But these aspirations were crushed by a mother who did not wish her daughter to have either professional or romantic ambitions, as Madge says: 'A seed is easily destroyed, but it might have grown into an oak tree' (Priestley 1994: 57). Neither of the two 'prodigal' daughters have become mothers and Priestley steers us towards thinking that Mrs Conway's version of motherhood – jealous, possessive, divisive and embedded in the fantasy of middle-class Edwardian grandeur – is no longer appropriate. As Lynne Walker pointed out in a review of a production of the play at the Royal Exchange theatre in Manchester, England, the game of charades played so enthusiastically and so exclusively by the family at the beginning of the play becomes a motif for the 'charade' of 'happy families'.[10] Priestley suggests that the social and economic imperative of the modern family unit is such that it needs to look outward to the world at large, rather than inward to its own closed and dysfunctional manifestations.

The Linden Tree (1947)

Just as *Time and the Conways* sees the return to the family home of two daughters who, although not exactly 'prodigal' in the same way as Stella in *Eden End*, have overt traces of prodigality, so too in *The Linden Tree* Priestley creates two returning daughters in Jean and Marion.[11] The sisters, now busy professional women, come back to the family home on the occasion of their father's sixty-fifth birthday: they have been called back by their mother who wants Professor Linden to retire against his will (see Chapter 5). What is interesting here is that Jean and Marion represent two extremes of the ideological spectrum. Marion has married into the French aristocracy and has become besotted with a social system based on clear distinctions between the classes and on the traditions of the 'Catholic aristocratic old world' (Priestley 1994: 230). Jean, on the other hand, is a doctor who, although an avowed socialist, despises the complacency of the working classes as well as wanting to make the world a fairer place in which they have more social and economic opportunity. For Marion, religion and the 'old civilised tradition' have helped her find an emotional equilibrium but as Professor Linden points out, religion has done little to benefit millions living elsewhere in the world. As far as he is concerned, she 'lives a very pleasant life', but not one which can 'solve a single major human problem' (Priestley 1994: 243). For Jean the 'peace of mind' which Marion has found in religion can also be found in the bottles of pills in her hospital. Religion is an escape and the 'best minds have always been fighting the churches tooth and nail. Just as they are today' (Priestley 1994: 268). She refers to love and romance as an 'old custom':

> And I hate all the idiotic feminine fusses and tantrums . . . what's the use of asking for a disciplined scientific society if I can't even discipline myself – a woman with a good scientific training.
>
> (Priestley 1994: 254)

Neither Marion's religion nor Jean's scientific disregard for the individual are shown as providing a way forward for Linden or for the world at large. Professor Linden's son Rex, who fought in the war and then played the money markets to great success, provides the route out of the life of a provincial university wife for Mrs Linden. Rex's attitude is cavalier, he calls it living by 'Spiv philosophy' – capitalising on the existence of a 'black market economy' – and unlike his father who does not wish to stop working, Rex believes that 'only mugs work' and that money provides a 'high wall or two and a little civilised amusement' (Priestley 1994: 251). As Mrs Linden decides that after years of marriage she will not wait for her husband to retire but will instead go to live in her son's lavish mansion, so the Linden family is effectively dissolved. The individualistic wins out over the communal and the ideological possibilities offered by either Marion or Jean are negated by Rex's belief that, with the possibility of another war and nuclear threat, individualism and the seeking of immediate gratification is the best option.

Patriarchy in crisis? *The Linden Tree* (1947), *Johnson Over Jordan* (1939), *Laburnum Grove* (1933)

For Hughes, *The Linden Tree* centres on Priestley's 'concern for the anxieties of individuals trying to drop anchor in the rough seas of a changing society' (Hughes 1958: 194). But Priestley's context for the individual is the family: the aperture provided by the family as a social unit, allows comment on the relationship between the individual and the social and political world in which they are located. While other plays examined in this chapter have focused on the changing dynamics of the feminine in relation to the family, Priestley simultaneously examines masculinity in a state of flux and patriarchy as no longer central to the family unit. Although not the only text which shows patriarchy in crisis and thus the traditional operation of the family under threat, embedded in *The Linden Tree* – with the threatened removal of the status provided by Professor Linden's job – is the link between patriarchy, employment and power structures within the family unit.

Linden's family has respected and benefited from his dedication to all things educational. His wife, however supportive on a domestic and emotional level, knows that he is unlikely to want to retire, and so manipulates a situation where the question of his retirement is brought to the top of the family agenda. No longer wanting to live what she has experienced as the isolation of life in a provincial university town, Mrs Linden initiates the deconstruction of Professor Linden's role as patriarch: if he has no job, or the limited status the university is prepared to grant him, and if she removes herself from the family home and takes up the option of a carefree life offered to her by her son, then Linden no longer has an on-site family to oversee. Rather, he is left to battle with the university over the nature of his future employment, keep watch over their teenage daughter and be 'looked after' by Mrs Cotton, the struggling housekeeper. Here Priestley leaves the patriarch to battle with his own conscience in a state of remove from the family over which he has hitherto resided.

Husband and father of two, Robert Johnson in *Johnson Over Jordan* (see Chapter 8) is similarly removed from his family. In the moments between death and some kind of afterlife, Johnson takes a journey through his past and is given the opportunity to re-examine the feelings and events which have shaped his life. Removed from his role as patriarch, he is somehow outside of time and has the privileged opportunity to witness his own family's responses to him as they go through the early stages of their mourning process after he has died. Moving between the distant and the recent past, Johnson comes to terms with how he has functioned as a husband and lover and as a father. His journey as a patriarch encompasses a 'return to the self', removed from a role within a social group back towards some attempt to understand his own individuality. We don't see how his role as patriarch has shaped his family, but we see how it has shaped his own life.

In both *Dangerous Corner* and *Time and the Conways*, the patriarch is very deliberately removed but the family is still somehow shaped by him in his absence. Thus in *Dangerous Corner*, Robert Caplan sees himself as carrying forward the family business very much on the same terms in which it was originally set up and operated by his father, but is stopped from doing so by the rupture which Martin's death, and the ensuing revelations about his life, reveal. Whereas in *Time and the Conways*, the father figure, again absent, has created an economic basis for the family but this is allowed to slowly disintegrate through mismanagement. It might be suggested that Priestley is offering some homage to the patriarch in these plays, but in fact what he is doing is far more complex. Just as Johnson is eventually able to unpick the fibres of his own existence through death and a journey to some sort of afterlife, so too Priestley invites a deconstruction of the ways in which the family as a collective group functions in a social and cultural environment in transition, through placing the patriarch in crisis or simply removing him from the stage.

In *The Glass Cage*, where no matriarch is present, it is the next generation with whom David McBane has to fight in order to sustain his position as patriarch. As the family secrets are exposed, so his children are exposed to the wider world outside of the tightly knit family, and in turn the community, from the centre of which he rules. The disjuncture of his belief system with the ways in which the family business has been run dishonestly, is a reflection upon the fact that his style as a patriarch is no longer tenable: he is forced to listen to and act upon the beliefs of the younger generation.

The patriarch, George Radfern, in Priestley's hugely popular 1933 play *Laburnum Grove*,[12] was played in the original London production by Edmund Gwenn, who also played Jess Oakroyd in the 1933 film of *The Good Companions* (see Chapter 6). An actor with a solid but quiet authority, Gwenn was perfectly suited to Radfern, the assured homely patriarch of an ordinary respectable suburban London family. As with many of Priestley's other comedies, the play is full of witty twists and caricatures of the middle class uncovered. Radfern's brother and sister-in-law are unwelcome and long-term guests in the family home, waiting for a hand-out from Radfern's hard-earned, well-saved money to give them the financial boost they feel they need to 'get on in the world'. Similarly, Radfern's daughter Elsie is besotted with a man who wants to borrow money from her father in order that he might buy into a partnership in a business. When Radfern, jokingly we believe, suggests that rather than working as an honest manager and businessman, he has, for some years, been laundering money with his old friend, Joe Fletten, the family are shocked. The unwelcome guests make a speedy exit and Elsie's fiancé calls off their relationship. Mrs Radfern is convinced that her husband has been fooling them with the suggestion that he is a criminal, and even an inquisitive visit by an inspector from Scotland Yard doesn't convince her otherwise. But Radfern's money printing business is no joke at all and the play ends with the family escaping their suburban existence to go abroad, and enjoy the fruits of Radfern's ill-gotten gains.

Here the suburban patriarch, in an environment which Tom Priestley has aptly proposed parallels the 'smooth underbelly of Mike Leigh territory' (Priestley 2003a: 10), takes his family away from 'ordinariness' and confinement of the nuclear family, but does so through criminality. What for Priestley was a veiled criticism of the British monetary system – as he suggests, 'the banks appeared to flourish when industry was failing' (Priestley 2003: 17–18) – *Laburnum Grove* is a celebration of the middle-class English eccentric male, well hidden beneath the veneer of suburbia. The family unit is not dissolved but rather, through the patriarch's inventive criminality, is removed from its almost repressive context.

Comedy, marriage and sexual relations: *When We Are Married* (1938), *How Are They at Home?* (1944), *Ever Since Paradise* (1947) and *Mr Kettle and Mrs Moon* (1955)

That Priestley was such an adept writer of comedy has, at times, been used as a justification for his near ejection from the English canon of twentieth century literature. Even relatively contemporary critics have found it difficult to place his comic writing alongside the more overtly politically driven works for the stage (see Innes 1992). Priestley's comedies – with a few exceptions such as *Bees on the Boat Deck* (1936, see Chapter 5), a thinly disguised farcical snipe at capitalism and its promoters – were among the more popular of his plays in production in England. It is, however, Priestley's populism which underpins much of the critical dismissal of his work (see Chapter 1). From a perspective of overview, it would be unwise to assess the impact of his oeuvre without paying attention to the comedies, and especially his comedies of marriage. With the possible exception of *When We Are Married*, in each of these – *How Are They at Home?*, *Ever Since Paradise* and *Mr Kettle and Mrs Moon* – Priestley investigates, through different narrative frameworks, the nature of romance, marriage and power relations between the sexes in sexual partnerships.

Late in life Priestley wrote very freely of his attitude to sex:

> I have been lusty and given to lechery and have never hidden my inclinations from my waking self. In other words, nothing has ever been suppressed in this department. Never a sexy inclination has been hurried out of consciousness. This does not mean that my waking life has been one long orgy – far from it – but at least it does mean that I have never been busy stoking the unconscious with a heated sexuality forbidden to consciousness. . . . I have come to terms with Eros while awake, so that, not neglected and furious, she has not had to burst into my dreams.
>
> (Priestley 1977: 105)

But the actual references to sex in the plays mentioned above are few and far between: sex is presented, through characters like the hilarious Monica Twigg in *Mr Kettle and Mrs Moon*,[13] as less important than the fraught but rewarding negotiations of actual lived relationships between the sexes. While Mr and Kettle and Mrs Moon turn to each other as they reveal their secret 'repressed' everyday selves, Monica is openly defiant of those who keep dismissing her from her varying places of employment because she refuses their sexual advances.

> MONICA: People think I am a sexy type – that's how I lose
>   jobs – but I am not so gone on sex. . . . All these pieces
>   in women's mags – they make me mad. All about what

you must do to find him and keep him. 'Make yourself fresh and dainty for him'. . . . Why don't they have a go at keeping fresh and dainty for *us*? And what do you get for it all? . . . four kids, a kitchen full of washing, red hands an' flat feet an' Housewives' Choice.

(Priestley 2003a: 216)

Her bright and breezy attitude is appreciated by Kettle, who sees her as wanting to escape the humdrum, respectable suburban existence which they both, from different perspectives, share. Kettle and Mrs Moon, having negotiated what each can expect from the other as a partner, ultimately leave the tedium of their lives as bank manager and wife-to-pompous-businessman and set off with Monica in tow, for the unknown and a life of relatively unconventional freedom.

In the earlier and better known *When We Are Married*, the three couples begin to reassess their marital relationships when they find out, while celebrating their silver wedding anniversaries, that in fact they have never been legally married at all. The power relations within the three different marriages all begin to shift as each couple wonders both what they might have done had they never married, and what they might do now that they believe they are in fact legally 'single'. Much comedy ensues as the balance of power within each relationship is transformed: behaviour tolerated previously is now frowned upon or simply deemed unacceptable. Eventually the couples are released from their turmoil and told they were in fact married after all, but we are left with a sense that their relationships will never be the same again.

A similar appraisal of romantic relationships is allowed through the framework of a wartime setting in *How Are They At Home?*, which ran originally for four months in London in 1944. Here Priestley sets up a number of romantic encounters among a group of wartime workers all gathered at the home of Lady Farfield, who has climbed the ranks and been promoted from the factory floor to a supervisory role. All classes are represented in the house as they gather for an evening meal, only to be constantly interrupted by the various officers and government officials who have been billeted to Lady Farfield's once ornate country mansion. While the butler has lost any sense of reality and is convinced that the house is still fully equipped with the requisite number of servants, Lady Farfield and her cook, a singer from the Vienna Opera, manage on wartime rations and a sharing of all resources. When an old flame, Edward Camyon, is billeted at Farfield Hall for the evening, he is convinced that Lady Farfield is still one of those people 'who can give parties every night, and fling money away, and keeps rows of servants waiting on them, and generally behaving like callous idiots' (Priestley 1949a: 409). Unaware of the truth as known by all the others, that she has 'given up her old privileges. No class distinctions. Democracy with its sleeves rolled up' (Priestley 1949a: 430), Camyon attacks her verbally for her presumed aristocratic ways inappropriate to wartime life. Offended by his lack of ability to see the reality of her domestic situation, Lady Farfield creates a charade of wealth and femininity with the other women and in doing so, exposes his blind pomposity and arrogance. Once he has realised the reality of the situation and begged her forgiveness, she points out that while the men are away at war, the women at home, 'work for them, pray for them and think of nothing else, deep down, but the time when it'll all be over and they're all back. And that's our real life (Priestley 1949a: 438).

Without the quietly romantic and distinctive class traces of Lady Farfield, Pauline is strong-willed, ideologically driven, assertive and sees sexual relationships in purely pragmatic terms. Working as a land girl she is practical and views relationships in terms of their functionality: assured that Tony is not the 'type of officer who is looking forward to nothing after the war but secretaryship of a second-rate golf club in a decaying society', she sweeps him off his feet. Rather than feeling threatened by her strident persona or her lack of traditionally feminine charms, Tony sees her as a 'girl' who has 'got everything' (Priestley 1949a: 436, 437). Thus Priestley sets up his 'topical' comedy as a means of examining relations between the sexes in a world turned upside-down by war: and here it is the 'new' women, masculinised to some extent by their circumstances who are endowed with the intelligence to lead sexual relationships forward. These are the same non-traditional women who Priestley problematises in the early essay noted at the beginning of this chapter – but here they are celebrated.

Priestley's *Ever Since Paradise*, which he subtitled 'A Discursive Entertainment chiefly referring to love and marriage' (Priestley 1949a: 443), is a pure and, according to Christopher Innes, 'ironic presentation of the battle of the sexes through Shavian debate' (Innes 1992: 367). Although comedic, the humour comes from the interaction of the characters' rather than from the context in which they find themselves. Creating what, at the time, were significant challenges in staging – two couples perform at the side and front of the stage, two play the piano at the sides and two 'perform' the history of their relationship from a stage within the stage – *Ever Since Paradise* shows Priestley in experimental mood.

Figure 3 Ever Since Paradise, New Theatre, London, 1947.
Photograph: Angus McBean. Courtesy of the Mander and Mitchenson Theatre Collection.

As Philip and Joyce bicker about each other's timing during the playing of the overture, so Helen and William begin to pull back the complex layers of their own relationship through examining the history of the faltering marriage of the 'stage within a stage' couple, Paul and Rosemary. Helen and William step in and out of the story – changing characters and playing different roles – and through doing so come to understand what may or may not have gone wrong in their own failed marriage. They are reconciled with the understanding that 'the sexual life is a cheat', and as Helen suggests, it is a cheat which 'takes us women in, just as it does you men'. The couple agree to 'share the cheat together – with humour and kindness – with trust and deepening affection' (Priestley 1949: 516). Priestley presents three couples as intellectual equals able to assess the dynamics of their marriages and identify the obstacles, either personal or cultural, which have lain in their paths. Dealing with what would have then been thought of as the primary familial relationship, that of husband and wife, Priestley echoes his early drama, *Dangerous Corner*, in using the theatrical possibilities of playing with time – reversing it, stepping in and outside of the past through storytelling and removing the realist framework. That *Ever Since Paradise* is theatrically more sophisticated than the earlier play is a credit to Priestley's engagement with the processes of theatre (see Chapter 2) as much as it is a result of the maturity of his playwriting. In releasing the temporal framework of a play from the unities of time and place and the boundaries of realism, Priestley challenges our perception of what we see and turns the 'domestic drama' into something more complex and theatrically challenging.

4 Time and the time plays

Time present and time past
Are both perhaps present in time future,
And time future contained in time past.
If all time is eternally present
All time is unredeemable.
What might have been is an abstraction
Remaining a perpetual possibility
Only in a world of speculation.

T.S. Eliot, 'Burnt Norton',
in *Four Quartets* (Eliot 2001: 3)

Time, space and the modernist sensibility

The construction of scientific and popular narratives about notions of time reached a highpoint during the modernist period, and especially so during the interwar years. Scientific and philosophical discourses around the nature of time were irreversibly influenced by a variety of innovations such as Einstein's theories of relativity, which had accumulated in the public domain by 1919. Einstein's theories were based on the supposition that time, space and distance are not absolute, and that their definition is relative and relational to context and observer. Such theories caused a seismic shift in the ways people thought about time and the individual's relation to the world and in turn the world's relationship to the universe. Others had similarly begun to investigate the relationship between time and motion as a means of assessing working processes and increasing industrial productivity: thus Taylorism, derived from the theories of F.W. Taylor based on time and motion studies in the workplace, became the basic tenet of mass production within industry, in which the production of goods was unimaginably increased by the introduction of the conveyor belt and the assembly line (see for example Taylor 1911). Charlie Chaplin, much admired by Priestley, famously deconstructed the effect of such 'mass' theories and working practices on the individual in his wonderfully insightful film *Modern Times* (1936).

Such scientific and industrial transitions were components of a culture in which the fixed nature of political and religious ideologies, economic foundations and social formations were already undermined: the catastrophe of the First World War left Europe, and Britain in particular, in a state of crisis and flux and the attraction of the 'immediacy of the modern' so praised by the avant garde, was combined with a loss of identity and a 'growing sense of dislocation and indeterminacy' among the majority (Parsons 2004: 175). Such transitions had already been set in motion during the late Victorian period, but the

> confident Edwardian world that approached war in 1914 had by now dissolved into myth, and, surveying its ruins, modern society faced a crisis of belief and identity.
>
> (Parsons 2004: 175)

For some cultural historians and critics, time, with its associations of memory, loss and the unknown, became such a 'dominant concern that it can be taken as a cultural signature . . . after the war . . . it became a fully thematised subject in its own right' (Levenson 2004: 197). After the First World War, there was no return to the 'known' world of peace, but rather a present and a future world which were unpredictable and alienating. This idea of a 'new world' is one which Priestley embraced to a greater extent in his plays during and after the Second World War (see Chapter 5), but during the 1930s and early 1940s much of his dramatic writing out of the issues around concepts of time – the loss of time, the compression of time and the reversal and recurrence of time – were predicated on the theories of mathematician J.W. Dunne and 'mystic' P. Ouspensky as well as on a belief that trying to understand the relationship between time, and individual and social responsibility, could create a society in which the individual and in turn the 'group', might flourish. Priestley's understanding that 'spatial and temporal practices are never neutral affairs' and that the 'instability in the special and temporal practices around which social life might be organised' (Harvey 1990: 239) produced by the interwar experience, was vital to the ways in which he 'played' upon and experimented with notions and possible definitions of time in his theatrical work.

Priestley and the culture of time

Priestley has a certain reputation which derives from his interest in time as a fourth dimension: known as the author of 'time' plays, his interest in theories of time expose a convergence of a number of other areas of thematic focus in his playwriting. Clive Barker suggests that Priestley was not alone in his dramatic experiments with time during the mid-twentieth century (Barker 2000: 230–1). The proposition that flashbacks, 'flash forwards and other cinematic techniques' were used by numerous playwrights 'to manipulate our responses by presenting alternative interpretations of what we normally experience as events happening in linear time' (Barker 2000: 230–1), refers, however, to the exception rather than the rule: Priestley was alone in his continuing obsession, on a variety of levels, with aspects of time in his playwriting. For other playwrights it was a fleeting contemplation, for Priestley it was a theme to which he returned from different perspectives, again and again.

Barker pinpoints the cultural significance of the varying non-linear/circular time theories prevalent during the interwar years: circular time – which merges past, present and future – allows for an avoidance of disaster as 'the moment of [its] happening will come round again', thus we can change our responses to events and alter our destiny. Equally however, if time is predestined then we don't have to take any responsibility for our actions (Barker

2000: 230–1). Priestley manipulated these two seeming oppositions in his 'time' plays, where often our relationship to time as
played out in the text is skewed or the characters experience time
in a form which places them 'outside' of time in terms of the
everyday and theatrical understanding of it. Similarly, his preoccupation with what would now be considered 'mystical' or
spiritually driven theories of time, which had a certain cultural
currency during the interwar years, meant that his plays often
demanded an engagement with questions around 'being' and
'becoming', a self-reflection about individual and social action
and responsibility. For David Harvey (1990):

> the opposition between Being and Becoming has been central
> to modernism's history . . . seen in political terms as a tension
> between the sense of time and the focus of space. . . . Even
> under conditions of widespread class revolt, the dialectic of
> Being and Becoming has posed intractable problems. Above
> all, the changing meaning of space and time which capitalism
> has itself wrought, has forced perpetual re-evaluations in
> representations of the world in cultural life.
>
> (Harvey 1990: 283)

For Priestley, the intersection of Jungian ideas, and the theories
of J.W. Dunne and in turn, P. Ouspensky, created the opportunity
to dramatise this supposed opposition between 'being' and
'becoming', whereby through presenting time as the fourth dimension, life narratives and the order of events can be questioned
and altered.

> We invent Time to explain change and succession. We try to
> account for it out there in the world we are observing, but
> soon run into trouble because it is not out there at all. It comes
> with the travelling searchlight, the moving slit.
>
> (*Man and Time*: Priestley 1964: 76)

For Grover Smith, Priestley was able, in his writings on time,
to demystify and 'illustrate the force of Dunne's speculations'
(Smith 1957: 224). Certainly, Dunne is given thorough treatment

in Priestley's *Man and Time*, written many years after his own 'experiments with time' in theatre. J.W. Dunne, originally a successful aeronautical inventor, was for Priestley, the most 'important figure in the campaign against the conventional idea of Time' (Priestley 1964: 244). His discovery and explanation of 'the displacement in time' in dreams lead to his rejection of the idea that our lives, 'are completely contained by chronological uni-dimensional time', and Priestley admired Dunne's ability to demystify propositions such as the notion that we can experience our future while in a dream state – thus our dreaming self cannot be 'contained with passing time' – and his suggestion that such possibilities are not reserved for the elite or the spiritually sophisticated alone (Priestley 1964: 245–70). Although cynical about some of Dunne's ideas and wary of the passive role given to Dunne's 'Observers' of time – that we observe different aspects of time and can articulate the observance of our observing *ad infinitum* – Priestley latched on to the idea of 'serial time' espoused by Dunne in *An Experiment with Time* (1927). In a theatrical context this allowed him to shift the relationship between what we see and what we understand ourselves to have seen in plays like *Dangerous Corner*, *Time and the Conways* and *An Inspector Calls*.

Playing with time: *Dangerous Corner* (1932), *Time and the Conways* (1937) and *An Inspector Calls* (1945)

Looking back in 1941, Priestley identified a sense that the world was already preparing for the rupture that would be caused by the Second World War by the mid-to-late 1930s. He stated that in 1938, 'even though the landslide had hardly begun, there was many a rumble, many a crack. . . . The time was out of joint (Priestley 1941a: 131). This feeling, that time is somehow 'out of joint', was one which haunted many writers during the interwar years (see Levenson 2004) and is reflected in Priestley's *Dangerous Corner*, albeit applied in a simplified manner (Innes 1992: 368). Considered by some critics as 'a shallow and contrived effort' (Skloot 1970: 426) and by Priestley as a 'trick thing' (Priestley

1962: 195) the plot turns around two devices, the first is that, as Priestley describes it, 'time divided at the sound of a musical cigarette box', both at the beginning and towards the end of the play (Priestley 1962: 195). Time is replayed and reconstructed as events from the past – the veracity of which are constantly in question – dominate the narrative. Thus at the point at which the identity of the music box comes into question in Act I (see Chapter 3), and Robert Caplan demands that the 'truth' of the family history be untangled from the charade of middle-class respectability, time moves between the present and the past, reconstructing each in our minds as it flows. Skloot (1970) also notes that as each act begins where the last left off, time is 'suspended rather than broken' and suggests that in fact here, Priestley is more interested in the 'tricks time can play' than with any actual theories of time (Skloot 1970: 428). As Act III of the play ends, so time is accelerated and we are sent back to the beginning of the play: the scene repeated from Act I has incidental text removed and here Priestley plays with our memory. We recognise the text and the stage picture from Act I, but, just as films on second viewing seem to be quicker because we have viewed them before, and so are waiting for things we know are about to pass to happen, so by the time we recognise we have returned to the beginning of Act I, the text appears to be moving faster and in fact, because of the omissions, it is. What we assume to be a gunshot implicating Robert's suicide, then appears to be the sound of gunshot which is part of the play the family are listening to on the radio – the same play they are listening to at the beginning of Act I. Innes reads the looping of Act III back onto the beginning of the play as a means whereby the

> naturalistic uncovering of dark secrets, and the acting out of violent crime, are nothing but an illusion, a *trompe l'oeil*. The classic detective story twist here is that the murder never happened.
>
> (Innes 1992: 369)

Alternately, one might read this twist as a rather clever theatrical device: we have witnessed what we then are unsure has actually happened. The hypocrisy and foul play has been exposed and explained and the idyll of middle-class comfort at the end of the play undermined, thus there is not the formal sense of closure traditionally promised by the well-made, three-act play. Smith suggests that in writing *Dangerous Corner* Priestley had already been influenced by Ouspensky's theories of time recurrence (see pp. 91–92) but in fact the play owes far more to the combination of the author's knowledge of the prevalent detective and thriller plays popular at the time (see Stokes 2000) and his desire to play with and challenge the form of the genre.

The device used in *Dangerous Corner* is reapplied later in Priestley's career with *An Inspector Calls* (see Chapter 7). Here, through his investigation into the death of Eva Smith, Inspector Goole forces the Birling family to scrutinise and account for their past actions, through reconstructing and altering their perceived relationship to the supposedly dead Eva. When in Act III the Birlings discover that Inspector Goole does not work for the police or any official agency and that in fact no one knows where he has come from, the implications of his investigations lose their immediacy for the family. However, the plot twists right at the end of the play when the family receive a phone call to tell them that an inspector is on his way to the house, to question them about a girl who has died from swallowing disinfectant. Birling has suggested that his daughter's feelings of 'Fire and Blood and Anguish', while under interrogation by Goole, are a sign that she 'can't even take a joke' (Priestley 1994: 220). This is of course completely undermined, as is our perception of the story, by the ending of the play. What we have been convinced was a hoax appears to have been some kind of premonition – Goole, as his name suggests, may have been 'unreal', but the moral turpitude of the Birling family is all too real. We are effectively, though not technically as with *Dangerous Corner*, being sent back to the beginning of the play.

The manipulation of audience perception was used again by Priestley in what is one of his definitive 'time plays', *Time and the Conways*. Here Dunne's theory of serial time, that we are all 'a series of observers' functioning 'in a series of times' (Innes 1992: 370) is more overtly applied as Priestley himself noted:

Suddenly I saw that there was a play in the relation between a fairly typical middle-class provincial family and the theory of Time, the theory chiefly associated with J.W. Dunne over which I had been brooding over the past two years.

(Priestley, quoted in DeVitis and Kalson 1980: 153)

The play takes the form of a well-made, three-act drama except that by reversing the chronology of the second and third acts, Priestley creates uncertainty as to the relationship between what we see happening on stage and its relation to 'reality'. Act I ends in semi-darkness with Kay's head '*silvered in moonlight. Very still she listens to the music, and seems to stare not at but into something, and as the song goes soaring away, the curtain creeps down*' (Priestley 1994: 33). At the beginning of Act II it appears that nothing has changed, Kay is in the same position at the window in semi-darkness, but then the lights come up and we see that the room has changed significantly and that we have moved forward to the present day (1937). Act II begins exactly where Act I ended although Kay appears changed: '*Something elusive, a brief vision, a score of shadowy presentiments is haunting her. She is deeply disturbed. She throws a look or two at the room, as if she has just seen it in some other guise*' (Priestley 1994: 62). We are back at the end of the birthday party celebrations from Act I, and just as Kay is uncertain whether she has been sleeping or awake and drifting into daydreaming, so we are unsure whether the events of Act II which have been played out before us were 'real' or not: we don't know whether time has made the seeming solidity of the family fall apart, or whether Kay has 'dreamed' her future. Act II ends with a conversation about time led by Kay's brother Alan.

KAY: . . . We've seen it tonight. Time's beating us.

ALAN: No, Time's only a kind of dream. . . . If it wasn't it would have to destroy everything – the whole of the universe – and then remake it again every tenth of a second. But time doesn't destroy anything. It merely moves us on – in this life – from one peep-hole to the next.

KAY: But the happy young Conways . . . they've gone . . .

ALAN: No, they're real and existing . . . We're seeing another bit of the view . . . – but the whole landscape is there.

KAY: But, Alan, we can't be anything but what we are *now*.

ALAN: No . . . it's hard to explain . . . suddenly like this . . . at this moment, or any moment, we're only a cross-section of our real selves. What we *really* are is the whole stretch of ourselves, all our time, and when we come to the end of this life, all those selves, all our time, will be *us* – the real you, the real me. And then perhaps we'll find ourselves in another time, which is only a kind of dream . . . You know, I believe half our trouble now is because we think Time's ticking our lives away. That's why we snatch and grab and hurt each other . . . I think it's easier not to – if you take the long view.

KAY: As if we're – immortal beings?

ALAN: . . . Yes, and in for a tremendous adventure.

(Priestley 1994: 60–1)

Numerous critics have pointed out that, here, Priestley makes direct reference to Dunne's theories: Kay observes the future of her family from a dream-like state in the present and is perhaps given the opportunity to intervene in order to change the envisioned future. DeVitis and Kalson note that what

Dunne contributes to the fabric of the work is a note of hope, an intimation of immortality . . . the audience is grateful for something to cling to in the midst of a life of pain. Pseudoscientific explanations are beside the point.

(DeVitis and Kalson 1980: 158–9)

Innes proposes that Dunne's theories 'offer support for the rejection of individuality as a subjective illusion' (Innes 1992: 370), it is certainly the case that if we read the presentation of the family in the play as a warning against middle-class complacency, then we can see the individual nature of the Conway family's conflicts as a reflection of and authorial comment upon a more general situation (see Chapter 3).

The play was highly successful during its original run (see Appendix) although Priestley was furious at the critical reaction which dismissed the theoretical underpinning of the play, an underpinning which one critic feels to be 'as dulling as when a figure or event in fiction must be accepted as unquestionably supernatural and not in any way an emanation of the character's unconscious fears or desires' (Chothia 1996: 108).

> That this theory should be hastily and contemptuously dismissed, by light-hearted newspapermen who had never given an hour's thought to the subject, seemed to me then, and seems to me still, unpardonable. With each of the Time plays, both in London and New York, many dramatic critics, with an air of vast intellectual superiority, produced observations that were childish.
>
> (Priestley 1941a: 123)

Dunne's theories had received serious analysis and had a certain currency among the general populace, and for Priestley his work was 'as important as it was at first difficult to understand' (1941). Critical reaction to Priestley's next play, *I Have Been Here Before*, was more enamoured with the way in which Priestley applied the combined ideas of Ouspensky and Dunne, perhaps because the plot creates more direct links to the more common time-shifting experience of *déjà vu*.

Dramatising time theories: *I Have Been Here Before* (1937)

Of *I Have Been Here Before*, Priestley later wrote:

> It is not – and was never intended to be – a play about rein-carnation. It is a play about recurrence, a theory I openly borrowed from Ouspensky's *New Model of the Universe*. Reincarnation says that we make many appearances, as many different personalities, in many different ages. Recurrence, as interpreted by Ouspensky, says we lead our own lives, with some differences over and over again. Actually I think that

reincarnation is perhaps a more attractive and more plausible theory than this of recurrence, but, I repeat, it has nothing to do with my play . . . I wanted to make dramatic use of the familiar but always eerie feeling that we have been actors in a certain scene before, of the sense, known to most of us though not all, of *déjà vu*.

(Priestley 1941a: 50–1)

It is interesting that the play was as successful as *Time and the Conways* in its original production, and that the basis of the theoretical propositions which Priestley worked into the plot was more 'spiritually' inclined than Dunne's. Ouspensky was a Russian émigré whose theoretical work about time and consciousness gained a devoted following among eminent literati such as Katherine Mansfield and emerging Jungian psychoanalysts like Dr Maurice Nicholl.[1] Priestley was not a 'follower' as such but was intrigued by Ouspensky's idea that the invisible or 'spiritual' world was accessible to the normal gaze through dispensing with the 'limitations of conventional logic', and that such 'invisible worlds' could be accessible to 'the higher levels of consciousness which man can develop if he chooses' (Reyner 1981: 6). None of this appears immediately to relate to Priestley as a socialist whose work was heavily influenced by his position on class and social action. However, it is important to remember that Ouspensky's work, for all its mystical qualities, was a reflection of a belief implicitly shared by Priestley, that mid-twentieth century man had become 'fractured or dissociated' and that this was a general as opposed to an individual position: Ouspensky did not believe that a return to 'normalcy' – a state of non-fracture – was possible, but rather that one 'could arrive at a higher self'.[2] Priestley saw the 'Work' which Ouspensky's followers undertook, as far removed from the tenets of the usual 'soft and sentimental doctrines of Higher Thought, Theosophy and the rest' (Priestley 1964: 264). The idea that man should rid himself of his automatic and mechanical reactions to the everyday world and operate on a more conscious level appealed to Priestley, who, although wary of the non-scientific nature of Ouspensky's writing (see Priestley 1964), nevertheless adopted and applied some of his ideas around the recurrence of time, which Ouspensky considered to be three dimensional – past, present and future converge at any given moment.

Thus in *I Have Been Here Before*, Dr Görtler is the outsider, a European émigré and an intellectual, within the English holiday weekend setting of a North Yorkshire village inn run by Sam Shipley and his daughter Sally. Thinking they are fully booked for the weekend, they turn Görtler away, finding it odd that he tells them he must have arrived in the wrong year, only to have their prospective guests cancel. Then Ormund and his wife arrive, take two rooms and we also meet Farrant, a school teacher at the school set up and run by a charitable trust funded by Ormund's business. Görtler returns, is given a room and makes numerous comments which imply that he has some detailed knowledge of the other guests. Görtler makes Sally 'feel uneasy in [her] mind' (Priestley 1994: 118) and she treats him as the unwelcome foreigner. Ormund engages in conversation with Görtler about his own past and his feelings about his horrific war experiences and, as he becomes steadily more inebriated from the whiskey to which he appears to be addicted, about his fantasies of suicide. Meanwhile, his wife Janet and Farrant spend the day out walking and somehow become besotted with each other.

As the play progresses, Görtler openly discusses his theories of time:

> time is not single and universal. It is only the name we give to higher dimensions of things. In our present state of consciousness, we cannot experience these dimensions spatially, but only successively. That we call time. But there are more times than one.
>
> (Priestley 1994: 123)

When Farrant sees Görtler's ideas as irrational, Ormund's response suggests that caution as opposed to arrogant dismissal would be wise on Farrant's part:

> Don't be too sure you know it all. Don't think you've got it all worked out. You bright young men, with your outlines of everything, are going to be horribly surprised yet.
>
> (Priestley 1994: 141)

Ormund, in whom Priestley wanted to represent 'the deep distrust of life felt by so many moderns . . . a man with a wounded psyche', is placed between 'a typically cock-sure young materialist [Farrant], busy over-simplifying everything, and a mystic . . . a deadly liability in a play' (Priestley 1941a: 50–1). Through his further discussions with Görtler, Ormund decides not to take his own life when Janet tells him she is leaving him, and his new found self-knowledge and sense of calm almost persuade her to stay. Görtler tells Ormund that his decision to live and begin a new and more positively framed life, not to 'return to the old dark circle of existence, dying endless deaths', but to 'break the spell and swing out into new life', is a sign that he has 'moved onto a new time track' (Priestley 1994: 152–5). In other words, Ormund lets his wife go freely with her lover and does not threaten her with financial ruin or public humiliation. Through this choice of action he becomes free to create his own future and the disaster which Görtler foresaw – that the pain of separation would leave all three, Ormund, Janet and Farrant in a state of collapse, is avoided.

For some literary critics the play remains an 'unconvincing melodrama' where the linguistic style awkwardly changes to fit the complexity of theory which it explores (DeVitis and Kalson 1980: 162; also see Atkins 1981). Others note that the heightened language at the end of the play is a necessary reflection of the fact that each of the key characters have moved away from their normative, everyday reactions to emotional challenges, that they are 'taken out of the commonplace' through engaging with Görtler's theories (Braine 1978: 80). The mainstream theatre critics of the time were less hostile than one might have expected and saw the play as an 'intensely interesting' attempt to explore the idea that fate is not inevitable, that it was, 'three times as exciting and five times as constructive as *Time and the Conways*'.[3] After this play, however, Priestley moved away from the exposition of time theories towards a more direct experimental manipulation of the theatrical dynamics and possibilities of time. In *Ever Since Paradise* and *Music at Night* he suspends, expands and reverses the direction of real time in parallel with the playing out of remarkably simple plot lines: we go inside the minds of the characters and this carries more importance than what actually 'happens' on stage.

The expansion of time: *Ever Since Paradise* (1947), *Music at Night* (1939) and *Johnson Over Jordan* (1939)

As a play, *Ever Since Paradise* relies on our voyeuristic desires to glimpse inside other people's marital affairs. Unlike *When We Are Married* (see Chapter 3), Priestley did not approach his subject here with an eye to formal comedy, although what he calls a *Discursive Entertainment* has many comic elements within it. The plot moves around the discussion by three couples, of the histories, and possible alternative histories, of their relationships. Priestley even parodies his use of Dunne and Ouspensky – the latter's work, thinly disguised, as being that of the well-known 'Madame Rubbishky' (Priestley 1949a: 490), as the couples discuss philosophical concepts relative to their situations and experiences. The dramatic frame is initially constructed around two of the couples, one of which provides musical accompaniment for the others, who act as narrators. But as Innes notes, 'the dramatic frame is increasingly broken' as the narrative moves us backwards and forwards in time (Innes 1992: 357). The fourth wall is removed for the audience, who are at times directly addressed and the linearity of the narrative is fragmented and broken into by Helen and William, the narrators who move in and out of the 'play' which is being acted out behind them by Paul and Rosemary – the character description for which is quite simply, *The Example*.

Time moves between real and reported time, in a non-chronological order, reflecting a dramatic technique 'extremely sophisticated' for its era (Innes 1992: 357). Innes argues that the play is structured around the idea of a hall of 'self-reflecting mirrors' whereby each of the couples reflects the historical relationship of the others – William and Helen, long divorced, see parallels between what happened in their own marriage and that of the couple they are 'reporting' on. Similarly Philip and Joyce, the accompanists, learn more about their relationship through witnessing and participating in the story of Paul and Rosemary. Time is stopped, repeated, replayed and projected forward.

For Innes, although a 'stylistic advance', Priestley's experimentation is here, 'under-cut by the comic clichés'(Innes 1992: 357), yet other critics have noted that the play has parallels with Brechtian technique.

> The Narrators, the episodic action, the shift from prose to verse, the endings of scenes revealed as they begin, the emphasis on *how* a relationship breaks down rather than *what* happens to the couple, the accent on the theater as theater all suggest devices of epic theater.
>
> (DeVitis and Kalson 1980: 176–7)

Although they also point to the fact that Priestley's is not a 'political' play, but one which reveals and asks for recognition rather than action. *Ever Since Paradise* is, however, a play in which Priestley chose to 'explore a universal theme in an experimental form, marking it as one of his most innovative pieces . . . the comedy is actually prophetic in suggesting another theatrical form which would soon be in vogue' (DeVitis and Kalson 1980: 176–7). Such experimental impetus was also key to *Johnson Over Jordan* (see Chapter 8) in which Priestley also attempted to remove normative structures of time from the play.

> What I wanted them [*Johnson Over Jordan* and *Music at Night*] to suggest was life outside Time as we usually know it, the kind of freedom of the fourth dimension that comes to us in a fragmentary fashion in dreams, events out of chronological order, childhood and adult life interrupting each other, all of which can bring a piercing sweetness, a queer poignancy, and, again, dramatic experience a little different from what one has known before.
>
> (Priestley 1973: 52)

For Innes, *Johnson Over Jordan* is more successful as an experiment because it presents the action 'from the perspective of a single protagonist who is central to every scene' (Innes 1992:

375). What is interesting about the play in terms of representations of time is that at key moments time past, present and future converge as Robert Smith makes his journey through his past at the same time as the chronology of time is deliberately blurred. The overarching framework – his funeral and the days which follow it – gives an added dimension to Johnson as the onlooker upon his own life: although he is in a dream-like state he also experiences the connection between the past and future and the present moment – he *is* in the office, he *is* in the nightclub and so on and while in these locations he is witnessing moments from his past while living in the present, albeit 'dream' time.

Priestley's use of deceptive time frameworks is repeated in *Music at Night*, a play originally written for the Malvern Drama Festival and produced in the West End in the same year as *Johnson Over Jordan*, but after the theatres had reopened, having been shut down at the outbreak of the Second World War. For Priestley, there are moments in the play which have the 'strange timeless poignancy of a dream' (Priestley 1944: vi); it is certainly the case that while the characters are listening to the new concerto written and played by David Shiel, we see them become 'half hypnotised into reliving the crises of their pasts' (Smith 1957: 229). Within the acceptable confines of a musical gathering in the household of an upper-class hostess, the mixture of people present is as representative of the British class system as it could be. Those such as the society reporter Phillip Chilham and the industrialist James Dirnie are literally haunted by ghosts from their working-class pasts. As the three acts, structured around three movements of the new concerto, progress, we play witness to the remembrances of the characters – the ghosts who visit do so in the actual present of the play and so the past is played out in the present as characters move in and out of their dream-like thought processes. Theatrically what we see involves very little physical movement – some characters move forward to speak, some speak from a static position as part of the on stage audience for the concerto. The 'action' is predominantly internal and as a result some have suggested that the play is dealing with the psychological conundrum of 'personality' (Rogers 1968: 15), while others liken it to O'Neill's *Strange Interlude* (1928) and read the play as representing the struggle with 'dead time' which many experience while listening to music (Smith 1957: 229; see also Skloot 1970).

The musical framework gives both unity to the setting and provides an opportunity to suspend time – the play lasts longer than a concerto would – and creates an atmosphere of 'other' time even though the text is full of contemporary references to the war – the Nazi regime and the aristocratic fascination with Nazism in a barely disguised reference to the Mitford sisters. We are taken back in time to 1920, to the First World War and the moment that hostess Mrs Amesbury's son was killed in an aeroplane, to Chilham's imaginary South Sea island and so on. The characters move outside themselves to represent people from the dreams of others on stage, or the voices of nameless groups of people. As the text moves in and out of specified time and geography, so the theatrical challenges of the play become more and more apparent: towards the end of Act III, the stage space transforms out of all recognition as the concerto draws to an end.

> the lights change so that the room seems to have vanished and we see a wide sky behind and in front of it two columns that might be part of some dateless temple. The whole effect should suggest humanity itself outside time. At the same time the dead should be grouped at one side, in such a way as to suggest there are countless numbers of them, that we are only seeing the beginning of a vast crowd.
>
> (Priestley 1944: 66–7)

Just as Priestley wanted to move the action from the 'surface of the mind to deeper and deeper levels of consciousness' (quoted in Evans 1964: 137) so too his utilisation of multiple locations and temporal references take us further away from the individualised specifics set up at the beginning of the play, towards a more 'universal' non-specified location as the play nears the end. In typical Priestley fashion we are brought back to the musical parlour right at the end of the play, to discover that Bendrex has died during the concerto and is taken away by the ghost of his manservant, Mr Parks.

Priestley's time plays, as well as exploring actual theories of time, also reflect his interest in the relationship between the individual psyche, aspiration and human potential. Theatrically they place him, especially taking into account the latter plays, alongside less 'popular' non-commercial playwrights more accepted by the modernist fraternity, such as Auden and Isherwood (Innes 1992: 377). The fact that Priestley was working in mainstream theatre where audience appeal had to be a major economic, and therefore artistic, consideration, did not stop him experimenting with form and ideology or from pushing at the boundaries of the audience's expectations of the theatrical experience: this is as much the case with his 'future time'/'utopian' plays examined in Chapter 5.

5 Work and visions of dystopia/utopia

> They will tell us we can't change human nature. That's one of the oldest excuses in the world for doing nothing. . . . We've been changing human nature for thousands of years. But what you *can't* change in it – . . . is man's eternal desire and vision and hope of making this world a better place to live in . . . – you can see this desire and vision and hope, bigger and stronger than ever beginning to light up men's faces . . . one here, one there . . . – until you begin to see there are millions of us – yes, armies and armies of us – enough to build ten thousand new cities.
>
> (*They Came to a City*: Priestley 2003b: 95)

Richard Dyer notes that 'two of the taken-for-granted descriptions of entertainment, as "escape" and as "wish-fulfilment"' point to its central thrust, namely, utopianism' (Dyer 2002: 20). Dyer is quick to note the oversimplified nature of such descriptions, far removed as they are from any traditional notion of cultural production which encompasses the utopian, but he rightly claims these loose terms as reflections of the fact that the 'utopianism' present in mass entertainment per se, 'works at the level of sensibility', presenting possible other worlds in a general sense rather than one which outlines 'ideal' worlds and how they might be organised (Dyer 2002: 20).

Both an informal and a formal embracing of utopias and utopianism are present in Priestley's work. Using theories of time in his plays and experimenting with actual time in theatrical time (see Chapter 4) could both be seen as active attempts to alter the relationship between the world as imagined and the 'possible worlds' implied, where the future is presented as changeable and the characters are given the opportunity to move towards their imagined ideal. More formally, however, in plays such as *They Came to a City* (1943) and *Summer Day's Dream* (1949), Priestley actually creates a 'utopian world' on stage, whereby the kind of dominant motifs of a utopian vision which Dyer notes George Kateb originally proposed, are debated:

> a world permanently without strife, poverty, constraint, stultifying labour, irrational authority, sensual deprivation . . . peace, abundance, leisure, equality, consonance of men and their environment.
>
> (Kateb 1972: 9, quoted in Dyer 2002: 25)

Beginning his playwriting career in the 1930s, Priestley was writing at a time when the post First World War economic depression created an environment of social flux, and he kept a sharp eye on the political scene as well as having a strong sense of the ways in which economics impacted on everyday life. As Holger Klein has pointed out, in earlier plays such as *Bees on the Boat Deck* and *Laburnum Grove* Priestley clearly condemns the world as is, heavily critiquing, albeit through a comic or farcical framework, the exercise of 'arbitrary private power'.[1] Priestley thought the country's financial developments should be managed centrally by the government, rather than being dependent on private individuals and investors who have only their own interests at heart. His call for a 'bourgeois democracy' was a reaction to the continuing concentration of real economic power among the ruling classes (Priestley 1941a: 241). However, he is clear, especially in his polemical work *Out of the People* – published as part of the Vigilant Books series which had the remit of 'dealing with the problems of reconstruction after the war' (Priestley 1941b) – that an alternative to the masters/masses dichotomy was urgently needed, that a 'better society' would not come from simply changing the class of those in power, but that the power structures themselves needed to be changed. Classing himself as 'essentially bourgeois and middle-class', Priestley wanted to change the balance of social and economic power between the 'producer of goods' and the 'lender of money' (Priestley 1941a: 241, 243).

> I am on the side of the workers, the masses (that most insulting term), the proletariat, but I do not believe that there resides in them some mystical virtue that will somehow become the leaven of a new and greater culture; just as I do not believe that the art of literature has taken an immense step forward because a few not very good novels about communal cement works have been published.
>
> (Priestley 1941a: 241–2)

Baxendale (2007) has noted the omnipresence of critiques of Priestley among recent historians of the modernists, where they accuse him of pandering to the petit-bourgeois, the 'shopkeeper classes', and in doing so offer a false reading of Priestley's appeal and political standing (see Baxendale 2007). Priestley's utopian vision of post-war reconstruction was in fact far more broad based and radical in its appeal. Writing in 1941, and without the political pressure faced during his BBC broadcasts (see Chapter 1), Priestley proposed that a 'vital democratic system' would benefit the whole of society, realising the potential of the individual and the community: the war provided an opportunity for crucial political change.

> This has happened before, when a class has newly come into power, and it is now time for it to happen again, but on a much bigger scale . . . because this time it is not an affair of one class being promoted to power but of the whole class system breaking down, leaving the people free . . . we are all the people so long as we are willing to consider ourselves the people, so long, in fact, as we put the community before any sectional interests.
>
> The collapse of the barriers and disappearance of the ramifications of the class system will act like the blowing up of a dam.
>
> (Priestley 1941b: 102)

The beginnings of such political change were to happen, to some extent, with the Labour landslide victory in 1945 and the implementation of the Welfare State a few years later. Priestley's plays make no grand call for revolution however, but consistently make reference to the ways in which the individual might recognise their social and political potential, whether in the private world of the family or the public world of work. Priestley did not imbue his plays with a 'message' in any crass sense, but his belief in human potential and possibilities for real social change colours many of them, especially those written in the late 1930s and 1940s.

In terms of Priestley's utopian visions, Raymond Williams's distinction of four 'types' of integrated utopian/dystoptian narrative is useful. Williams groups these as the paradise, the externally altered world, the willed transformation and the technological transformation (Williams 2005). Priestley does not move towards the former 'paradise' until *They Came to a City* and *Summer Day's Dream* but the other three definitions are all pertinent to earlier plays which deal with critiques of capitalism all framed in terms of the experience of professional life.

The meaning of professional life: *Bees on the Boat Deck* (1936), *The Linden Tree* (1947) and *Cornelius* (1935)

'Professional plays' whereby the dynamics of office life, running a small business or even choosing between whether one worked for a company or took the risk of working for oneself, had a certain currency on West End stages during the interwar years in particular (see Gale 2004a, 2004b). But Priestley's emphasis is on the relationship between professional life, personal ideology and individual psychology within a framework of cultural transformation. Thus in *Bees on the Boat Deck*, 'a clever attempt to reduce the political scene to terms of farcical comedy' (Hughes 1958: 160), Priestley critiques a structure in which economic planning was 'based on human expediency and human effort was grossly wasted' (Evans 1964: 162). Here Gridley and Patch are in charge of looking after the no-longer seaworthy *S.S. Gloriana*. The play contains the deliberate introduction of a variety of social 'types' as the plot by the owner – helped by his exploitation of the naivety of an onboard scientist developing explosives – to destroy the ship and collect the insurance money is foiled by the two comic leads. Gridley and Patch undermine the plan but not because they are anti-capitalist per se, they simply want to work in a world in which they know where they stand and, on a professional level, one in which their hard work is recognised and rewarded. In response to the communist party worker Gaster for whom 'Our first duty is to the revolution, the proletarian state, the real community', and capitalist owners are culpable for all wrongs, Gridley points out, 'it's not just a case of the have and the have-nots' (Priestley 1949a: 136). When Gaster suggests that those who made the ship are the real owners, Gridley cynically tells him,

> Most of 'em wouldn't know if they were making a ship or a skating rink and wouldn't care . . . I don't want a party, yours or anybody else's. I don't care about capitalists and proletarians, masses and bosses. . . . I want to see some men about, real men who know what sense is and duty is and order is.
>
> (Priestley 1949a: 137)

Priestley deliberately places his two comic leads among a number of ideological polarities: Lord Cottingley, the capitalist, Gaster, the communist, and Captain Mellock, the fascist. In doing so he allows them to explore the politics of their working lives – they choose a philosophy of honesty, hard work and duty as the means by which they might find professional and satisfaction.

Gareth Lloyd Evans is critical of the way in which Priestley placed his political analysis inside a comic framework, feeling that ultimately the themes are 'exploited for ends which contradict them' (Evans 1964: 164), but this is to ignore the powerful relationship between comedy and political critique. Audiences, despite the presence of rising stage stars Ralph Richardson and Laurence Olivier in the cast, were equally unimpressed by the play, which ran for fewer than fifty performances. The depth and frequency of overt ideological statements in the play may well have lacked appeal for audiences who thought they were going to see a 'farcical tragedy' – but for Priestley this play on genre was deliberate: a strong political analysis embedded in a farcical framework. Clearly the world in which Gridley and Patch function is dystopian, but Priestley gives them the potential to effect change through action. This presentation of a hero in the face of a society transformed, with the potential to stand his ground and battle with the injustice brought about by the 'politics' of professional life, found more resonance with audiences in Priestley's later play, *The Linden Tree*, produced after the Second World War, when audiences were far more directly affected by the political sentiments which Priestley lampooned and critiqued in *Bees on the Boat Deck*.

The Linden Tree's Professor Linden, a university teacher who has lived a life of relative privilege, is faced with overcoming the new regime running his provincial university. Much to his wife's disgust, he left Oxford University to work in Burmanley, which is now in the virtual control of Dr Lidley, a 'high pressure educationalist', a successful 'director of education in several cities' (Priestley 1994: 228). Linden's work environment has, in Williams's (2005) terms, undergone a 'willed transformation' leaving his vision of a utopian educational environment – where students are nurtured and encouraged to think for themselves – in a dystopian state. Of Lidley, Linden notes, 'He educationalizes – in quite a big dashing sort of way. It's something quite different from educating people – newer and much better. They'll probably have machines to do it soon, when they can import them from America' (Priestley 1994: 254). Lidley represents the drive for non-individualised learning, turning universities into educational factories, whereas for Linden education should be moulded to individual need. Even though he is of retirement age, Linden wants to fight against the university authorities and carry on working, despite his professional environment metaphorically having 'a pinched look, frayed cuffs and down-at-heel-shoes', he prefers to stay, to be part of the 'crew' as opposed to a passenger, to 'help a bit if I can' (Priestley 1994: 283). Although he admits that his son Rex's ability to make money may be something he secretly craved himself, Linden is left behind in Burmanley when his wife chooses to go with Rex and live a life of gentile and luxurious retirement. Thus Linden, whose workplace is less and less like the mirror of Oxford University which he would have liked it to become (Priestley 1994: 228, 247), chooses to continue his contribution to the community. Just as Williams points to the interconnectedness of utopian and dystopian structures, so too Linden makes the decision to battle inside a negative environment for a more positive one. This struck a chord with post Second World War audiences of the original production, which ran for over 400 performances, with a cast including theatrical icons Sybil Thorndike and Lewis Casson. Hughes (1958) suggests that this may have been because Linden's is

> the bewildered eye through which a changing society is viewed, analysed and finally understood; and his children are the guinea-pigs of that society, each of them representing a typical post-war reaction and displaying the dangers that particularly threaten a world in need of red-blood and hard-headed courage.
>
> (Hughes 1958: 204)

The play corresponded to a very specific 'culturally and histori-cally determined sensibility' (Dyer 2002: 21), but it is interesting that in reviews of a recent production at The Orange Tree theatre in London, critics alluded to the fact that Linden's sentiments are as relevant nowadays as they were after the Second World War. The *Guardian* reviewer found it to be the 'most topical play on the London stage', while the reviewer for the *Evening Standard* claimed that the play probed all the 'anxieties of our modern, progressive middle class' and the *Daily Telegraph*, not know for its leftist stance, reviewed the production as speaking with 'extraordinary freshness to our own pessimistic age'.[2]

The struggle to deal with external change as part of an attempt to find satisfaction in the work environment was also the under-lying theme of *Cornelius* (1936), an earlier, less successful play.[3] Performed to pre-war audiences, and subtitled 'A Business Affair in Three Transactions', the text makes frequent mention of the economic context and deals with the effects of the collapse in foreign trade, the transformation of business methods – no longer personalised but catering to more competitive mass markets – and the changing relationship between both business and the economy and, as a result, the individual and the experience of professional life. Cornelius is running 'Briggs and Murrison' in the absence of Murrison, who is scouring the country for new contracts in a faltering economic climate. As the play progresses, Priestley presents different attitudes to work in the variety of characters who are employed in the office: Miss Porrin and Mr Biddle, the two long-term and loyal employees, are pitched against Lawrence, young, ambitious and looking for more rewarding work elsewhere. Cornelius's belief in the ability of Murrison to save the firm slowly disintegrates as meetings with creditors and Murrison's seeming mental breakdown on his return, make it obvious that the company will not survive. Realising that society does not necessarily provide rewarding employment for anyone willing to work hard, Cornelius is faced again and again with the possibility that the world is 'closed' to some and we are all in fact like 'bees in a glass cage' (Priestley 1936b: 24). As he states:

> I've always had at the back of my mind a little open door, with plantations and jungles and pampas and quartz mountains just outside it – with the sun on 'em. Don't tell me that all the time that little door's not been open, has been locked from the outside, screwed fast.
>
> (Priestley 1936: 24)

At the end of each act, Cornelius refers to a book he is reading on South America and fantasises about the adventures he might have there as an alternative to the professional life he is embroiled in. By the end of Act III, his utopian vision of the Andes provides escape from the option of suicide taken by Murrison: while the others condemn Murrison's choice, Cornelius points to suicide as a positive way out,

> they won't have life on any terms. We will . . . we linger on and on in the bit of light that's left – calling it *sticking* it –

when all the time we are simply frightened of the jump into the dark.

(Priestley 1936: 60–1)

Cornelius takes this 'jump' in choosing not to commit suicide himself after the firm has gone into receivership at the end of the play. He throws away the revolver he has pensively been handling, hurls the ledger so hard against the door it is smashed open, and leave the stage while speaking, 'jerkily' but with 'gathering force', words from his book about the Andes, 'we decided to take the track into the clouds – to find – amongst those heights . . . the lost city of the Incas' (Priestley 1936: 70).

With its poetic ending, *Cornelius* shows glimpses of the imagery in the later *Johnson Over Jordan* (1939): Cornelius is a different kind of 'everyman' to Robert Johnson, but there are similarities in the ways in which each uses the immediacy of their present situation to recapitulate on their pasts and re-evaluate their possible futures (see Chapter 8). Although there is a sense in which characters such as Mrs Porrin and Biddle represent a longing for a bygone world, any element of nostalgia is firmly undermined by Cornelius's ability to analyse the present: one small business cannot turn around the economic climate, nor can it halt progress – the 'Enormous offices, all glass and metal and light, open at ten and closing at four' of the future (Priestley 1936: 61). Nevertheless, he chooses not to be just a cog in the machine of commercial business. Cornelius chooses an individualist path, whereas for Professor Linden in *The Linden Tree*, the community still has potential. Similar choices face the characters in Priestley's later 'utopia/dystopia' plays, all of which suggest possible worlds transformed by historical events.

Urban visions of utopia: *They Came to a City* (1943)

Priestley conceived the idea for *They Came to a City* from the early days of the war, but it was not written until 1942. A play which explicitly reflected the 'hopes and fears and sharp differences of opinion about the post-war world of various sections of the British people', the original production ran for 280 performances in London, mirroring the popularity of the numerous productions which appeared countrywide (Priestley 1944: vi–vii). For Evans, Priestley had a 'calculated design upon the audience' and the play is a 'sincere piece of propaganda for Priestley's belief in the perfectability of man' and his 'unabashed vision of Utopia' (Evans 1964: 193). DeVitis and Kalson make more of the fact that with it Priestley 'accurately gauged the mood of a nation at war' and poignantly, that we are given very few details of the actualities of the Utopia he creates on stage (DeVitis and Kalson 1980: 194–5). It is certainly the case that when the characters describe what they have found in the city outside which they mysterious arrive in Act I, very little real detail is given. What comes across is the atmosphere, the attitudes of the people in the city, and brief glimpses of their reported activities. The geography and architecture of the city are implied through the setting, Priestley's opening description of which is very specifically detailed (see Priestley 2003b: 20). The set is architectonic and lacks any curvature – it is stark and imposing. We never see the city itself and the passing of time is given pictorial dynamic through lighting, which Priestley specifies should move through dawn to daylight, sunset and dusk through shades of grey, blue and purple with bright daylight streaming through the city doors when they first open.

During Act I the characters, all representing a range of classes – a few from the ruling class, a banker from Leamington Spa, a merchant seaman, a cleaner and so on – do not know where they are or how they have arrived there. By the end of Act I all have entered the city and Act II is devoted to their reactions to it. The ruling classes and financiers – Lady Loxfield, Sir George and Cudworth – and the petit bourgeois characters such as Mrs Stritton – do not like what they have found in the city. For them the dancing in the city gardens, the lack of interest in wealth, the equality between the city dwellers, has little appeal. Mrs Stritton, wife of the banker from Leamington Spa, even goes so far as to say that she hates the city, where people 'don't know how to behave properly' and 'everybody pretends to be as good as everybody else!' (Priestley 2003b: 80). Her husband, who aspires to

Figure 4 *They Came to a City*, The Globe, London, 1943.
Photograph: John Vickers, London. Courtesy of the Mander
and Mitchenson Theatre Collection.

more than their safe middle-class life, loves the city where 'They
have some people – great thinkers, scientists, artists – that they
admire and respect and look after better than we do any of our
really great people' (Priestley 2003b: 80). Of the nine characters
who filter on to the stage in Act I, those who do not like the
city find the comparative classlessness within its walls hard to

comprehend or admire. Conversely, for Joe Dinmore, the disillusioned ex-seaman, the city offers a level of equality which he
had only hitherto imagined: he admires the 'social justice' so
obviously present and this is what also attracts Lady Loxfield's
daughter Philippa (who felt she 'came alive in the city'), Alice the
waitress and Mrs Batley the cleaner – to whom the citizens offered
comfort and looked after for once in her life. Although Joe wants
to stay in the city with Alice, he also wants to tell as many people
as possible that the city exists, and so he and Alice are the last to
leave the stage to spread the news about the city where

> Men and women don't work for machines and money, but
> machines and money work for men and women – where greed
> and envy and hate have no place – where want and disease
> and fear have vanished forever – where nobody carries a
> whip. . . . Where men . . . have come out into the sunlight.
> And nobody can ever darken it for them again. . . . 'I dreamt
> in a dream I saw a city invincible to the attacks of the whole
> earth, I dreamt that was the new city of friends'.
>
> (Priestley 2003b: 95)

Full of idealism, some have criticised the play for being
'magnificent sermonising' (Agate 1946: 84) and for being peopled
with social stereotypes (see DeVitis and Kalson 1980; Hughes
1958), but the characters are functional and subservient to the
thrust of the play's argument which concentrates on the possibility
of an ideal new world in the face of the old world crumbling. For
Priestley this was a 'work of "symbolic action" concerning
different attitudes of mind toward postwar change' (DeVitis and
Kalson 1980: 196), and it is among his works which present real
theatrical challenge both in terms of style and composition,
condensed into two acts whereby all action is reported and implied.

Rural visions of utopian futures: *Summer Day's Dream* (1949)

Summer Day's Dream is set in the future 'post-Third War' world
of 1975. With their 'utopian' existence forced upon them through

historical circumstance, Stephen Dawlish and his extended family live on an old country estate now run as a farm. They exist by growing their own food and bartering with neighbours in an England so much reduced by the devastation of war, that the nearest thing to a 'capital' is what remains of a small market town. Dawlish and his family spend their days tending the land and simply surviving in a world stripped of luxury. Despite this they are content and have come to rejoice in the fact that they no longer have time for anything that 'doesn't either feed our bodies or refresh and rejoice our spirits' (Priestley 2003b: 142). The pastoral idyll is firmly interrupted by the arrival of three members of the new dominant world powers – Heimer from 'American Synthetic Products', Irina Shestova from the Russian government trade department and Dr Bahru, a scientist working for the Indian government. These three represent the world as was, the continuing dystopia out of which Dawlish's utopia was ironically made possible. The presence of the three reminds Dawlish and his family of what it is they have gained through their lifestyle borne of disaster, as they are threatened with the possible destruction of their landscape by Heimer's company, who plan to appropriate the land and set up a factory city for the purpose of extracting valuable deposits from the land. For the three foreigners such extraction represents progress and is inevitable, for Dawlish and his family it is a reminder of all the horrors of twentieth century existence which they were forced to leave behind. As Dawlish points out, the commodification of his land for the purposes of industry is nothing but another opportunity for Heimer and his kind to 'drive blindly on and drag the rest of us choking in the dust behind you' (Priestley 2003b: 151).

The play is replete with discussions about the merits of industry versus husbandry, of nature versus science, and the ending, whereby the interlopers, so moved by the rural utopia and so convinced by the dedication of the Dawlish family to this 'alternative' to their 'first world' existence, tell their respective superiors that the land will not provide the commodity they had originally thought it would. They return to their world of 'TV-Comms' and 'atomicars', and Dawlish is left with his little bit of non-capitalist, non-technology dependent utopia.

For some the play 'disarms criticism' with its 'languorous, dreamlike setting' although Priestley ultimately falls into 'woolly-mindedness': the political message is embedded in an emotional one about the power of love and the attraction of the rural idyll (DeVitis and Kitson 1980: 212–13). One critic of the original production wondered if it was in essence a short play somewhat overworked and overwritten, is seen as a reason for its relative short run in the West End (Atkins 1981: 222).[4] Some critics, however, saw the play as locating Priestley alongside Orwell and Huxley in his ability to visualise future and dystopian/utopian worlds.[5] Priestley's ideological proposition, whereby a world based on profit at the cost of the comfort or happiness of humankind, is pitched against an imagined one where there is equality and harmony, is present in many of his plays but none more so than the previous two plays discussed and *Home is Tomorrow*.

Political dystopia/utopia: *Home is Tomorrow* (1948)

Produced in 1948 and running for fewer than forty performances,[6] *Home is Tomorrow* is a provocative play in which Priestley suggests that technology and social development might help improve the lives of the inhabitants of an imagined under-privileged South Caribbean island, 'Corobana'. DeVitis and Kalson point out that this is ironic in terms of what the slightly later *Summer Day's Dream* offers as a view of technology (DeVitis and Kalson 1980: 213), but both plays present an analysis of colonisation in very different contexts.

Edward Fortrose is employed by the United Nations Under-developed Territories Organisation (UNUTO), an organisation which has the United Nations at its centre. His team of officers, doctors, scientists and administrators is attempting to introduce proper medical care and education to the islanders who have been hitherto exploited by various European colonisers. As he imposes UNUTO values on the islanders, so those native to the island with a more radical agenda try to block his team's work. Fortrose is drawn in sharp ideological opposition to his wife.

JILL: . . . I only hope UNUTO is booted out of here before they have abolished all fiestas in favour of discussion groups and shows of those dreary little films about inoculating babies and canning pineapples.

(Priestley 1949b: 46)

Others of his workers reveal their own prejudices as the two-act play progresses – Melnik suggests that the only way to deal with the radical nationalist Vezabar is to have him 'liquidated', and Riberac accepts a bribe from Lerma, the Director of Pan-American Alloys, who is also trying to get Fortrose to come and work for him. We are led to believe that Vezabar wants his home island to belong to and be governed by its own people, but then we discover that he is on Lerma's payroll. Fortrose discovers what Lerma has known all along that the island is full of rare beryllium minerals, from which his company can make an unimaginable fortune. Fortrose reminds Lerma that the Corobanains will revolt against his imposed mafiaesque regime, headed by Vezabar and that they will eventually fight back, that given a choice they would rather work with UNUTO. However, financial power and violence prevail and Fortrose is murdered by Lerma's henchman Vezabar in the closing moments of the play.

Home is Tomorrow is a clear moral condemnation of the dominance of economic imperatives over equality, although the play is lacking the critique of colonisation which present-day audiences would demand – the native islanders are either violent or aspire to be like the colonisers. It is, however, a very progressive play in its predictions of the heinous aspects of globalisation and the increasingly questionable role of international government organisations such as the United Nations. Priestley was, however, criticised for never letting his characters 'off duty', their construction always functioning to ideological argument (Hughes 1958: 206) in a play where he 'telegraphs his plot-line' (Evans 1964: 202). Atkins suggests that the 'defeat of the international ideal by political gangsterism' does not solve the issues which Priestley raises, but notes that these issues have a continuing relevance (Atkins 1981: 221). Whatever the specifics of the ideological questions which the play raises, it has in common with many of Priestley's plays, whether utopian/dystopian or not, the conviction that class or cultural division is no excuse for humanity not to engage with and thrive upon the benefits of community as opposed to individualism; albeit that the community may be carved out of both a frustration with existing political structures and an individual disquiet about one's relationship to society at large. The solidity and frequency of this conviction have given his plays a continuing currency which Part III of this volume, by examining a variety of his plays in production, explores.

Part III

Key plays/ productions

6 *The Good Companions*

J.B. Priestley's 1929 novel *The Good Companions* created a whole new public profile for the writer: it became a bestseller not long after publication and found its way into the nation's affections on a level neither Priestley nor his publishers could ever have predicted. As Priestley noted:

> This idea of a picaresque long novel aroused about as much enthusiasm as a stuffed walrus at an exhibition of water-colours. The long novel was out of fashion, expensive to print, hard to sell. The picaresque was out too, except perhaps as an excuse for fancy dress.
>
> (Priestley 1962: 181)

Selling millions since original publication, *The Good Companions* has also been adapted for the mainstream, for numerous small-scale productions worldwide and for screen and for television, with the original film, in 1933, launching the celluloid career of the then sweetheart of the British musical stage, Jessie Matthews. Both the novel and the various performative versions and adaptations have, since 1929, found a continued cultural resonance with audiences.

In the late 1920s and early 1930s, the British public were just beginning to come to terms with the devastation, both emotional and economic, of the First World War when the Wall Street Crash in 1929 brought fears of economic depression and decline back onto the agenda. *The Good Companions*, with its strongly embedded sense of community and message of hope and optimism, caught the zeitgeist and became *the* novel everyone was talking about:

> the total advance sale was only about 3,000 copies. The book cost 10s. 6d., a stiff price for a novel in 1929 . . . we thought, 7,000 or even 8,000 might be sold. . . . The book came out in July and for weeks nothing much happened. . . . Towards Christmas the daily sale was more than the total advance had been.
>
> (Priestley 1962: 183)

The success of *The Good Companions* was a mixed blessing (Braine 1978; Cook 1997); Priestley was now perceived as a 'bestseller' and looked down upon by the highbrows (see Chapter 1), or bemoaned by popular readership because he had not followed up the novel with another written in a similar vein: people found it hard to accept that because he had written 'one, jolly, hearty, popular novel it does not follow that everything I have written since ought to be exactly the same' (Priestley 1940: 7–8). As Braine suggests, the novel 'marked the emergence of Priestley as a name and as a myth', and to some extent the 'myth' of Priestley as *merely* a populist is still with us (Braine 1978: 26; see also Baxendale 2001).

The Good Companions follows the fortunes of Miss Elizabeth Trant, Jess Oakroyd and Inigo Jollifant as they go in search of challenges beyond their previous everyday lived experiences. Miss Trant, a spinster from the upper-middle classes, uses her inheritance to fund her transition from the closeted and thankless life she has led looking after her ailing and now deceased parent. Jess Oakroyd is made redundant and decides to leave his unhappy marriage and family life to seek work elsewhere in the South of England. Inigo Jollifant, a teacher at a low-grade, old-fashioned boarding school, volunteers to leave his employment when castigated by the headmaster's wife for illegally playing the piano after hours. The three converge through their meeting up 'on the road' and their engagement with the misfortunes of a travelling concert party, The Dinkie Doos, who Miss Trant offers to bail out of debt and then manage. The company goes from strength to strength, with Jess working as a stage manager and carpenter and Inigo finding his voice as a composer. He also finds love in the form of Susie Dean, the company's ambitious and talented lead singer-dancer. The story ends as Miss Trant refinds an old flame who is now a doctor, Inigo finds success by selling his compositions to a musical impresario in London, who also gives Susie Dean a starring role in a London show singing his songs, and Jess, after the death of his wife, sets off for a new life in Canada with his emigrant daughter and newly born grandchild.

Such a brief outline of the plot does little to show the intricacy and dynamic of the narrative, which is full of an extraordinary range of characters – criminals, fairground workers, landladies, salesmen, school teachers and solicitors as well as performers from different generations and theatrical contexts. The novel is divided into three parts, the first of which sees the main three characters drawn from a diversity of class and geographical contexts, brought together in the middle of England. Convergence through diversity lies at the centre of the novel, which is predicated on the idea that whatever their background, the characters are all in search of something which will make them members of a self-defined community. They have all lived isolated lives in pre-determined contexts and through 'making' theatre they are brought together, regardless of background, in pursuit of a common goal.

The novel's detailed descriptions of the landscape and its inhabitants are echoed in Priestley's journalistic tracts such as *English Journey* (1934), which he called his 'rambling but truthful account' of his observations of a journey through England in 1933 (Priestley 1934). *The Good Companions* gives a real sense of England in the late 1920s and early 1930s: as Braine suggests, we look at England through the characters (Braine 1978: 38). The novel ends with an Epilogue 'addressed to those who insist upon having all the latest news', and in this way Priestley simultaneously acknowledges the appeal of the characters he has drawn and leaves the text open to the possibility of a follow-up novel, which of course was neither planned nor written; he is merely playing with our desire to keep the characters alive in the active imagination.

Braine defines *The Good Companions* as almost the 'arche-typically well-made novel' and suggests that Priestley here manages to 'combine complexity and richness with simplicity' (Braine 1978: 29), whereas Atkins and others rather dismiss it and construct its literary importance around the myth that it gave Priestley financial stability for the rest of his career (see Atkins 1981; Klein 1988). The novel certainly gave him, in his mid-thirties, an opportunity to further explore other forms of artistic expression that were more financially precarious than journalism – such as playwriting. The success of the novel and the subsequent performative adaptations – both those actualised and those planned but never made – indicates that *The Good Companions*, centred on theatre as an enriching and community-building experience, and has an archetypal character and appeal, the various dynamics of which this chapter goes on to examine.

KEY PRODUCTIONS

Production I: *The Good Companions*, 1931 – from page to stage in the West End

The Priestley and Edward Knoblock stage adaptation ran at Her Majesty's theatre for over 300 performances. A very long production run for its era, it was one of only three of his plays which ran for over 300 performances in their original London productions – the other two being *Laburnum Grove* (1933) and *The Linden Tree* (1947). Although Priestley states that his 'arrival' in the 'London Theatre' came in 1932 with *Dangerous Corner*, he had already been part of the team which created a hit in *The Good Companions* in May 1931. The fact of the play's success would have given him both professional and economic immunity from the 'fastidious minority' who so critiqued his populism in writing the novel (Priestley 1977: 47), and a significant level of marketability with West End managements. The play makes no attempt to pander to limitations of location or casting and as such would have been expensive to produce. The text has a similar episodic quality to the novel and is divided into two acts and fifteen scenes, demanding fourteen different sets on stage. Using two real vehicles, a cast of thirty-seven plus numerous extras, this was a large-scale production, the launching of which played on the continuing success and popularity of the novel.

The text is multilayered and emphasises the geographical landscape of the story. A greater percentage of the characters are drawn in an in-depth manner than in the later film versions which tended to focus on the central four, Oakroyd, Trant, Jollifant and Dean. Some of the play-script does find its way into the 1933 Gaumont British version, but has a richer quality replaced in the film by the different signifying possibilities of the medium. The stage adaptation allows for a stronger development of characters such as Mitcham, the well-travelled performer and conjurer or the travelling salesmen and market people – Jackson, and Linoleum Man and the Envelope Man – with whom Oakroyd spends time before he meets up with Miss Trant in scene 6. The stage adaptation maintains the textual variety of the novel, making full use of regional accents and echoing the novel in creating a very strong sense of the different characters through which the story unfolds.

Inigo's speech in which he decides to join the troupe towards the end of Act I, scene 8, a turning point in the play, drives the narrative forward and takes us from talk of action to action itself in Act II, which focuses on the work of the troupe in rehearsal and on tour.

> INIGO: . . . I'm not sure what a trouper is, but I'm jolly glad to know that I am a good one. If it means being a good companion, then I'm proud to be called one – . . . there isn't too much – er – good companionship left in this world, is there? Everybody – well, not everybody, but a lot of people – are out for a good time – and that's alright of course. . . . But it's nearly always their own good time and nobody else's they're out after isn't it? . . . An awful lot of hard nuts about now.
>
> (Priestley and Knoblock 1935: 47)

Figure 5 The Good Companions, His Majesty's Theatre, London, 1931. Courtesy of the Mander and Mitchenson Theatre Collection.

Not only does the speech find Inigo coincidentally formulating the name for the troupe under Miss Trant's management, but also it states and confirms the political agenda behind the plot. Whereas Gareth Lloyd Evans suggests that *The Good Companions* is 'in form' a projection 'from the basic concept of the family circle as the seminal organisation for the perfect state', it is in fact more complex than this (Evans 1964: 21). The 'family' as created in the play is non-traditional and extended well beyond the bounds of a functional family unit. Priestley is replacing 'family' with 'community' whereby members of the community choose to be so, and choose to work toward a common goal. This suggests that the text has an underlying radical agenda for which Priestley is rarely given credit. Reviews of the production also suggest that the sense of community reverberated with audiences, many of whom would have come to see the play because of the familiarity and cultural status of the novel.

Critical reception

> Alone among civilised mankind I seem to be the only person who has never read Mr Priestley's celebrated novel. This neglect brought its own punishment last night, when in the theatre I sat feeling like a tragic outcast, or like one who finds himself among a crowd of good people to none of whom he has been introduced.
>
> As every character familiar to those who have read the book appeared on the stage there were shouts of delighted greeting and happy recognition . . . so the play starts with the enormous advantage of having a ready made public eager to see their favourites step out of the printed page.[1]
>
> I had no idea just what a classic 'The Good Companions' has become. Every character, every incident and every joke were greeted by a rapturous audience like an old friend.[2]

Most of the production reviews are framed by the play's original form as a novel. *Punch* joked about the fight between Priestley and Knoblock over which aspects of the novel to keep and which to sacrifice, and suggested that the audience were not interested in the play but merely in the relationship between the play and the original novel.[3] The reviewer for *Time and Tide*, a small circulation journal aimed at the middle-class intelligentsia, warned 'highbrows' about the effusive theatricality of the piece.[4] Other reviewers critiqued the production as a poor *play* but a good *stage show*, in other words, it was not the traditional fare defined as a 'play' but more like a musical comedy; critics did not know how to place it.

The reviewer from *The Times* was less concerned with definition and more generously recognised that the form derived from the content: 'This is the theatre all out, and thank heaven for it; there was never a better occasion for a strong whiff of grease paint, an abundance of wise barnstorming and music to taste'. Ignoring the populist appeal of the production, he equally praised the 'firm, rapid narrative' and saw it as a 'dashing piece of *bravura*'.[5] Ivor Brown, who was later to become a good friend of Priestley's, reviewed the play in terms of the fact that it 'attempts no more and achieves no less than' entertains, reflecting the way in which reviews of the play were overshadowed by critical agendas which separated out 'good plays' and 'good theatre'.[6] That the production was somehow the latter was seen in either negative or rather patronising terms. Reviewers resentfully noted that the production would have an extended run: resentment was a reaction often inherent in the appraisal of much of Priestley's work – a rather perverse critical response to popular success.

Production II: from stage to screen – *The Good Companions*, 1933 – Gaumont British and Victor Saville

Following on from the phenomenal success of both the novel and the stage version, Gaumont British bought the rights of *The Good Companions*. 'Talkies' were still relatively new in 1933, and a whole generation of audiences were still more familiar with the idiosyncrasies of silent movies and the way meaning is created visually rather than aurally. Nevertheless the film capitalised on the success of the stage version, using Edmund Gwenn – a celebrated stage actor who later worked in a number of Priestley productions – as Oakroyd and the original stage Inigo Jollifant, John Gielgud. After much searching Jessie Matthews was cast as the rather hard-nosed and ambitious Susie Dean – and when Priestley refused to 'soften' the role, she complained that he had written Dean in such a way as to imply that he didn't like women (Thornton 1974: 101). Gaumont British had employed their young 'ace' director Victor Saville to work on the film and invested substantial amounts of time and money on scripting the adaptation and screen-testing actors. Thornton (1974: 97) suggests that as, 'a property, *The Good Companions* was very much the studio's *pièce de resistance*', an investment which subsequently paid off at the box office.

Saville's film plays on the geographic breadth of the novel: the opening is framed by a map of England, the pieces of which are removed like a puzzle to reveal the central characters and their locations, Oakroyd in Bruddersford, Jollifant in the Fens and Miss Trant in the Cotswolds. Each of the three are spoken to by an invisible narrator, who opens the film with the statement that this is a film about the 'roads and the wandering players of England'.[7] Bruddersford is visually signified through filmed sequences of industrial buildings billowing out smoke, and mill workers at work, then crowding through the factory gates on their way home, to the sound of the noisy clickety-clack of the factory machinery. In contrast, the camera sweeps across the sleepy Cotswolds where the fields are full of peaceful and well-fed livestock. Throughout, with shots of trains overlaid by changing bill posters advertising 'The Good Companions', we are reminded of the swift transitions of the novel. The narrative is driven in part by the constant change of location, the speed of which slows down as the film progresses and we focus in on The Dinkie Doos/The Good Companions, at the point at which the plot turns; as they move from struggle and relative failure to success, so the landscape becomes more permanent. Saville makes use of montage and overlay and creates a visual feast of England in the early 1930s, from the North West, through the English Midlands to the glamour and bright lights of London's 'theatreland'.

The script focuses on the romance between Susie Dean/Jollifant and briefly, Miss Trant/Doctor McFarlane. Thus it attempts to appeal to a 1930s female audience, now voters and professionals, in a number of ways. Dean is ambitious and professional – she is not only driven and independent but also romantic. Similarly, Miss Trant chooses excitement and adventure when her father dies and leaves her a small income: when her solicitor suggests that she supplement her income by becoming a lady's companion, she refuses and tells him she is going to spend the money and set off 'into the blue'. These are portrayals of spirited women, who are independent, adventurous, ambitious and romantic as well as professional. Although Matthews had wanted Priestley to soften her attitude to Jollifant, Susie Dean comes across as mature for her age and far less self-absorbed and self-centred than in the stage and the later film version. Her relationship with Trant is as colleague to colleague not simply boss and worker, and it is she who brings Trant together with her former admirer McFarlane towards the end of the film.

Saville's 1933 film has a number of interesting performances, from Gielgud, not a film actor at this point, but one who plays

Figure 6 The Good Companions, film directed by Victor Saville, 1933.

the lightness of Jollifant with a real command of comic timing, and from Max Miller as Milbrau, the talent scout who speaks faster than Jollifant can think. The film draws to a close with Susie Dean dancing a short glitzy sequence – strangely reminiscent of Josephine Baker – and starring in a West End review and then ends by implying a further expanded geography, as Oakroyd sets off to visit his daughter in Canada. Made at a point when the mass film industry was still relatively new and open to experiment, *The Good Companions* capitalises on the novel's complexity of plots and the centrality of its depiction of the changing landscape of England in the late 1920s and early 1930s.

Production III: *The Good Companions* adapted – J. Lee Thompson's 1957 film

J. Lee Thompson's 1957 film of *The Good Companions* is the most removed from the original of all the versions. Shown only a few times on terrestrial television since its first release, and hugely extravagant in the vein of 1950s British musicals, the film was not as successful as the producers had hoped. Thompson, in choosing to update the setting to the 1950s, loses many of the subplots and creates little of the sense of the community so prevalent in the original versions.

Thompson's was one of less than a dozen British musical films released in the 1950s, others of which, such as Val Guest's *Expresso Bongo* (1959), were more tuned in to the emerging post-war, recently post-rationing youth culture. Conceived in 1953, but not produced until significantly later, the context of production and release is important. The film portrayed a different set of 'cosier' values not shared by young audiences of the 1950s, living in a world very different from that of their parents.[8] The destruction of the Second World War and the resulting threat of nuclear war, the disappointment felt by many at the relative failure of the post-war Labour landslide government and the emergence of a new 'angry' youth culture, meant that the film was shaped around an imagined world which no longer had such cross-generational appeal. However, as evidence of cultural history and of the ways in which a text is adapted for screen, Thompson's version of *The Good Companions* offers an interesting range of possibilities.

The film centres on the rise to fame, through a combination of hard work and romance, of Susie Dean. The part was originally conceived by the studios for Audrey Hepburn, who was then bought out of her contract by an American production company, at which point the project was shelved for a few years. Once revamped, the film starred Janette Scott as Dean,[9] John Fraser as Jollifant, Celia Johnson as Miss Trant and a host of young British performers such as Anthony Newley, Rachel Roberts, Shirley-Ann Field and Alec McCowan, who went on to make names for themselves in British stage, film and television during the 1960s and 1970s. With the removal of many of the subplots, the script is weakened by its focus on the few: elder characters such as Miss Trant/Celia Johnson are left with very little in the way of script. This is a film about a youthful love affair and a performer, Susie Dean, who is on the ascent.

The integration and disintegration of the performance troupe is shown in a far more heightened way than any of the previous adaptations, and although the film makes heavy use of the stage as location – backstage, in the wings, in rehearsal and so on – the finale, with its lavish song and dance numbers is filmed mostly head-on and plays on filmic technique – the illusion of a *stage* performance is almost entirely removed.

There is a visual acknowledgment of Priestley's desire to move the narrative around England – the film opens and is punctuated by a steam train speeding along a track over an estuary in the distance – but we are not given the sense of the breadth of the geography of England so integral to the 1933 film version. Thompson takes the troupe back to Bruddersford for the finale and so Jess's story comes full circle. Here he finds Mrs Oakroyd/ Thora Hird (dead at this point in the original), who at first castigates him for working in a theatre troupe then changes her mind and supportively joins in the scuffle on Susie's benefit performance night. Other characters are equally 're-formed' in the film. Lady Parlitt is no longer the stout aristocrat but a very friendly and giggly Joyce Grenfell who, after her somewhat incongruous marriage to Jerry Jerningham – young, athletic and rather camp – saves the day by taking Jerningham, Dean and Jollifant into her dead husband's theatrical production company and launching them in the West End.

Although the film has a very episodic structure with some thirty-seven scenes, which are predominantly backstage, onstage or in and around the theatre building, it loses the rhythm of the previous versions in part because of the deletion of a number of the subplots and the limiting of the geographical variety of either the novel or the first stage and film versions. The film begins with the assertion by a booking agent that The Dinkie Doos are old fashioned – the manager of the Royal Theatre, somewhere in the English Midlands, asks them if they have 'ever 'eard of striptease, rock and roll or the talking pictures', and so sets up an expectation of nostalgia. Thompson plays on a combination of traditional popular performance styles and those more current in the 1950s – so 'Mitcham's Magic Kitchen' is juxtaposed to Rachel Robert's sexy cabaret solo played seductively to the camera towards the end of the film, while Janette Scott's finale performance is reminiscent of the big song and dance numbers in films like *Gigi*. But the attempt to recontextualise *The Good Companions* to the

1950s somehow failed, even with textual insertions such as Milbrau's 'Anybody can write a concert, but it takes a composer to write a pop!' The film loses both the novel and stage versions' sense of community built and sustained and replaces it with an attempted focus on youth culture and romance.

Production IV: *The Good Companions* adapted – Previn and Mercer – the 1974 musical

I was not concerned directly with *The Good Companions* as a musical . . . but of course I took a semi-paternalistic interest in it. The music and lyrics by André Previn and Johnny Mercer seemed to me . . . very good indeed, quite exceptional; and if they were coolly received by some sections of the press, I think it was because it was thought that two Americans shouldn't be involved in our very English *Good Companions*. After playing to enormous money at Her Majesty's for some months, it began to slip during the lean weeks after Christmas and was then whipped off to make room for another musical that proved to be a disaster. Had it been nursed for a few more weeks – as many a long-running musical has been – it would not only have run on and on but would also have been presented overseas. It remains in my mind as an ambitious and loveable musical that deserved more loyalty from its management.

(Priestley 1977: 79–80)

Previn and Mercer's 1974 musical, starring Judi Dench, John Mills – surprising critics with the agility of his show-stopping tap dance in the latter stages of his career – and Christopher Gable,[10] was an attempt to find 'a style for a British musical which is successful and entertaining but . . . not in any way an attempt to emulate the American shows'.[11] Although a critical success and playing to full houses, costs could not be overcome by the small post-Christmas audiences and the management were not prepared to invest for a long run. Thus, even in the 1970s Priestley's earlier criticism of the management structures within the industry still had relevance.

With lyrics by Johnny Mercer, who had penned such hits as *Moon River* and *Fools Rush In*, and music by André Previn, the then conductor of the London Symphony Orchestra, the production was directed by Braham Murray, an up-and-coming ex-Oxbridge director. Priestley was involved from a distance in the production and was unhappy with various aspects, such as the detraction from the three main characters caused by the opening song and dance numbers. He did not like the casting of Susie Dean and felt that the actress Marti Webb was 'short of feminine charm'.[12] Priestley was in his eighties when this production was mounted and although Ronald Harwood, who had written the 'book' for the production, was a friend, the tone of Priestley's correspondence around the production process is marked by his sense that his advice wasn't quite being taken seriously. Interestingly, reminiscent of the opening shots of the 1933 film, he wanted a large map of England to be the first thing the audience saw. Although the Previn/Mercer production was largely faithful to the novel, using the temporal setting of the late 1920s and early 1930s, promoting the importance of the troupe and its community with such opening numbers as 'Camaraderie', 'We haven't got a tuppeny piece to buy a cup of tea, but we've got – camararderie!',[13] it was created by a young team, few of whom would have shared Priestley's experience of the era of the original.

The production ran for half a year and was well received by critics, who to some extent shared the perception of *The Good Companions* as sentimental and nostalgic. Although a number commented upon the ways in which the success of the novel had reverberated through British culture over some forty years and beyond. Although less successful, Alan Plater – credited with numerous British television hits from the 1960s onwards – adapted the novel into a nine part series for ITV in 1980. For Priestley the story had remained so popular because it was a 'fairy story' which comes right in the end, but one which was written with a background which was 'one hundred percent accurate'. The appeal of *The Good Companions* must also be accredited to its creation of a self-defined and inclusive community which struggles against adversity, a community focused on maintaining 'a great rapport between audience and performers'.[14]

7 *An Inspector Calls*

During 1945 Priestley campaigned vigorously for the Labour Party, although he himself had stood unsuccessfully as an Independent candidate in a Conservative stronghold (Brome 1988: 281–2). His socialist belief – non-politically party specific – in the need for post-war social reconstruction is mapped directly on to the First World War (1912) setting of *An Inspector Calls*. One of Priestley's best known and most popular plays, it is a political parable where the social and ideological concerns facing the contemporary post Second World War audience are located inside a historical setting.

> BIRLING: We employers at last are coming together to see that our interests – and the interests of Capital – are properly protected. And we are in for a time of steadily increasing prosperity . . . And I say there isn't a chance of war. The world's developing so fast that it'll make war impossible. . . . We can't let these Bernard Shaws and H.G. Wellses do all the talking. We hardheaded practical business men . . . we've had experience – and we *know*.
>
> (Priestley 1994: 165–6)

> INSPECTOR GOOLE: . . . there are millions . . . with their lives . . . all intertwined with our lives, with what we think and say and do. We don't live alone. We are members of one body. We are responsible for each other.

> And I tell you that the time will soon come when, if men will not learn that lesson, then they will be taught it in fire and blood and anguish.
>
> (Priestley 1994: 207)

Priestley plays on the word 'ghoul': for Goole haunts the Birlings, refusing to let them forget their past actions and forcing them to take responsibility for their effect on those from whom they have been socially isolated. Inspector Goole is drawn in overt ideological contrast to Birling, who espouses individualism: 'a man has to mind his own business and look after himself and his own' (Priestley 1994: 168) places him at the opposite end of the ideological spectrum. The anti-capitalist perspective of the play was not new in Priestley's work; in earlier plays such as *Cornelius* (1935) and *Bees on the Boat Deck* (1936) he had directly questioned the ethics of capitalism as an economic framework (see Chapter 5). But it was in his plays of the 1940s, and especially in *An Inspector Calls* – a deceptively conservative one-set, well-made play, where the action all takes place over one evening – that Priestley most clearly stated his humanist and socialist ethics.

The play is set in 1912, a week before the sinking of the Titanic, a ship which for successful industrial manufacturer Mr Birling signifies the height of technical advances capitalism has made. The temporal setting is a device, so that we are taken back to the Edwardian period in order to show us that the social and moral choices made in the present, 1945, are not dissimilar to those which Goole makes the Birlings face up to in the imagined past. Birling refuses to accept the inevitability of war in Europe, while the premiere audience would have just emerged from the throes of the 1939–45 war and may equally have lived through the 1914–18 war which Birling is so insistent, in 1912, could never happen. All the action takes place in one location, the Birlings' dining room which they occasionally exit but which we, the audience, never leave. We hear about the outside world, but the physical world in which the characters operate becomes, as the play develops, more distant from it. The central 'character' of the 'single mother' Eva Smith, around which the plot unfolds, enters the stage world only through the inspector's revelations about her life and the Birlings' role in her tragic demise – we never see her.

The play opens as Birling and his family are seated around their dining table, having finished a meal in celebration of Sheila Birling's engagement to Gerald Croft. Mr Birling expresses his excitement that his daughter's engagement brings together the two successful business families – the Crofts represent an established and moneyed upper-middle-class 'old county' family. Birling's 'festive fat forecasts' (Klein 1988: 201) inform his daughter and future son-in-law that by 1940 they will be living in a world which has 'forgotten all these Capital versus Labour agitations and all these silly little war scares' (Priestley 1994: 166). He is clearly drawn by Priestley as a man who, from the perspective of an audience in the mid-1940s, is in denial about the realities of world affairs.

The celebration turns sour when Inspector Goole arrives and begins his inquiry on the family's involvement with Eva Smith who, according to the inspector, has committed suicide by swallowing strong disinfectant. Slowly the family are all shown to have had a significant relationship with this woman: Birling was her employer until he dismissed her because of her suspected role in strike action and Sheila had her dismissed from the shop where she had found work, because she thought her impertinent. We then discover that Gerald had met Eva Smith, who by then had changed her name to Daisy Renton, and had befriended her, letting her live in his friend's flat and giving her money. The friendship turned into a romance and when Croft eventually broke off the affair, Eva then became involved with Eric Birling and found herself pregnant with his child. When she then went to the local charitable board to ask for financial assistance, her request was turned down by Mrs Birling – chairwoman of the organisation – who took a dislike to her, believing Eva had given herself 'ridiculous airs' (Priestley 1994: 199) by refusing to accept money or marry the father of her child. Through the inspector's questioning, the whole family become implicated in the girl's suicide, but all except Sheila and Eric refuse any responsibility for this.

By the end of Act II Mrs Birling has realised that the man most implicated is her own son: that he stole money to support Eva and that she has unwittingly suggested that he be publicly punished for doing so. In Act III Gerald tries to reverse the story when he finds out that Goole, who by now has given his last speech and left, is neither an inspector nor an employee of any law enforcement agency, and that the hospital have not admitted any suicide cases that day. At this point we see the reinforcement of the generational split, the beginnings of which were visible from the opening of the play: Sheila and Eric Birling feel responsible and are shocked by their parents' lack of sympathy for Eva. Sheila can't believe that they are acting as if nothing has happened: 'Everything we said had happened really had happened. If it didn't end tragically, then that's lucky for us. But it might have done' (Priestley 1994: 219). The final slant happens right at the end of the play when Birling, busy telling them all that the inspector was a hoax and there is nothing to worry about, takes a phone call in which he is told that a girl has died on her way to the hospital having swallowed disinfectant and that an inspector is on his way to begin his inquiries. Thus the play ends by returning to the beginning of the plot. Priestley's circularity implies that we are being taken back to the beginning of Eva's story in order that the Birlings might once again be made to take responsibility for their social actions.

Critical reception

Although the play has gained more cultural significance in later years, it was not one of Priestley's most successful with British theatre audiences when it was first produced in 1946. Critics such as Ivor Brown (1957) hardly mention it, whereas others point to the criticism that

> it was no surprise to the audience to know Inspector Goole did not exist. They had known all the time that it was Inspector Priestley . . . the danger lurking in the play – [is] that it may become a lecture in Civics by the author.
>
> (Pogson 1947: 48–9)

Although some literary critics judged it to be one of Priestley's 'tautest, best constructed dramas', they felt that he 'awkwardly injected the play with contemporary relevance' and preached at the audience, no longer trusting their 'intellect or intuition' (DeVitis and Kalson 1980: 200–4). Other critics took a more positive attitude to the play and noted a similarity with *Dangerous Corner* (1932), his earlier play which made use of the thriller/detective trope (see Chapter 3), but felt that with *An Inspector Calls*, Priestley 'cut hard with a knife' in order to implicate the audience as well as the fictional characters (Hughes 1958: 199). For Evans (1964: 184) the play was the 'clearest expression' of 'Priestley's belief that "no man is an island" – the theme is guilt and social responsibility'. Atkins (1981), however, has commented that the play was

> so well constructed and at the same time bears such a deeply felt social observation, where a fundamental realism is tempered by just the right degree of mystery and symbolism, that it is hard to fault the play in any way.
>
> (Atkins 1981: 217)

Similarly, other more conservative writers like Noël Coward admired the play's construction and its surprise ending.[1]

Considering the play's production history, it has received remarkably little attention from literary critics or theatre historians: this is in part a response to its perceived simplicity. But its simplicity is rather deceptive: Priestley not only makes use of the detective formula but also plays with our sense of time and reality. He creates a central character who never appears and whose existence we are encouraged to dispute in Act III of the play. *An Inspector Calls* seems to have suffered until recently in Britain from its origins as a text deeply embedded within a form of socialist ideology which was informing radical thinkers in the 1940s: most of the criticisms of the play, even those made by his colleagues, were based on the fact that Priestley had supposedly used it as an opportunity to 'preach politics'. Priestley, like many other left-wing writers during the period in which the play was conceived, wanted a social and political shift which took Britain forward to a society based on equality and community after the Second World War, not backwards to the class-ridden society of the Edwardian period. That this belief is reflected in the play has not stopped it from being performed on a surprisingly continuous basis, all over the world since the mid-1940s. It may also be the precise reason for its relative critical neglect. As John Braine has pointed out, 'audiences have not found it difficult' as a play (Braine 1978:115).

KEY PRODUCTIONS

Production I: Tairov at the Kamerny Theatre, Moscow, 1945

Alexander Tairov was one of Russia's foremost directors, founder and 'chief director of the Kamerny (Chamber) Theatre in Moscow from 1914–1949' (Worrall 1989: 15). Worrall places him alongside Diaghilev and Meyerhold in terms of his contribution to 'theatrical "modernism" in Russia' (Worrall 1989: 3). Tairov's reputation was founded not only on his aesthetic experiments in state-funded Russian theatres, but also on the basis that he promoted Western European and American drama in Russia. Having directed Priestley's *Dangerous Corner* in 1940, he turned to *An Inspector Calls* in 1945 as part of his search for the 'best of the most "progressive works" of world drama' (Worrall 1989: 71). He directed the play with his associate L. Luk'yanov.

Priestley's reputation in Russia had been strengthened by productions of *Dangerous Corner* and *Time and the Conways*, but his very 'definite anti-fascist position during the war, his radio talks, in which he showed himself a passionate advocate of the United Nation's cause', also enhanced his authority and popularity there (Drieden 1945: 25). British relations with Russia were politically strained but Priestley was one of a group of British writers and intellectuals who actively engaged with a process of promoting understanding between the two nations (see Priestley 1946). Unable to find a London venue for the play, *An Inspector Calls* (renamed *He Has Arrived*) received its premiere in a communist Russia barely out of the turmoil of the Second World War.

Figure 7 An Inspector Calls, directed by Alexander Tairov, Kamerny Theatre, Moscow, 1945. By kind permission of the J.B. Priestley Collection, The University of Bradford, from a commemorative album of the Priestleys' visit to Russia in 1946.

The Tairov production set the mode of design for the later London production:

> The directors and the artist E. Kovalenko emphasised the significance of the image of Goole on the first appearance of the inspector on stage. In the big room of the Birlings' flat, it was semi-dark and only the table at which they were gathered on the occasion of the daughter's engagement was brightly lit. But Goole comes in and the whole room becomes lighter, the footlights get brighter and brighter, illuminating all the corners of the stage space, and the light, intensifying, takes on shades of flame, the scarlet colour of retribution, the colour of anger and fire.
>
> (Golovashenko 1970: 138)

Tairov used the device which director Stephen Daldry was later to employ and develop, namely, Inspector Goole's costume was from the 1940s not the Edwardian period: he chose not to 'adhere

Figure 8 An Inspector Calls, directed by Alexander Tairov, Kamerny
Theatre, Moscow, 1945. By kind permission of the J.B.
Priestley Collection, The University of Bradford, from a
commemorative album of the Priestleys' visit to Russia in
1946.

to the literal concreteness of time and action'. This was done in
order to show that 'those social conflicts which the drama and the
destruction of Eva Smith have defined remain part of our culture'
(Golovashenko 1970: 138, 139): Tairov wanted to use Goole's
costume as a means of signifying a clear connection between the
social and political choices of 1912 and those of 1945. The
Birlings' dining room table dominated the scenic space; for Tairov,
Priestley had 'seated a whole world around a dinner-table, while
in the destinies of each person he makes you feel the breath of
larger social strata, societies and states' (Drieden 1945: 25).
Tairov's *An Inspector Calls* was not a detective play but a
'psychological play about morality, conscience, addressed to
"ordinary" people' (Drieden 1945: 25). Goole was the inspector
of the 'human conscience'. He becomes a judge in what Russian
critic Boyadzhiev saw as the 'court-room'/bourgeois dining room
within the Birlings' home:

Figure 9 *An Inspector Calls*, directed by Alexander Tairov, Kamerny Theatre, Moscow, 1945. By kind permission of the J.B. Priestley Collection, The University of Bradford, from a commemorative album of the Priestleys' visit to Russia in 1946.

The external aspect of the production, the movement of the action itself can be interpreted as a strict and impartial court. The manorial dining room of the Birlings is transformed under our gaze into a . . . court-room. The table standing in the middle of the room is almost an executioner's block and the four chairs arranged at the sides, the defendants' benches. The course of the court is inexorable. One by one the guilty stand up and confess to their crimes, and each time the directors find a bright expressive arrangement dictated by the internal dramatic state of action. The *mise en scene* of this production is a model of theatrical plastic art.

(Golovashenko 1970: 139)

Tairov's interpretation was very much in accord with post-war Russian socialist thinking: Goole was not a representative of the state apparatus but rather the 'voice of the people'; yet Goole remains a complex figure, 'not simply the accuser'. He did not only 'expose, but . . . also suffered from the fact that people are imperfect, that the world in which he lives is so unjust and cruel'.

The actor playing the inspector was required to portray a man of 'great humanism – demanding and impassioned': for Tairov, Goole had come to the Birlings' from the wider 'strata of society – like a democrat, like a socialist' (Golovashenko 1970: 139).

Production II: The Old Vic – the London premiere, 1946

The first London production of *An Inspector Calls* ran for fewer than 50 performances: this is in contrast to the first production of the play in post-war Germany, which ran for over 1600. Priestley notes this production without giving any detail, only to mention that he received negligible royalties (Priestley 1962: 195). One should, however, note the different reactions of post-war audiences to the play: the English were less moved by the proposal that the individual take responsibility for their actions than the Germans.

The 1946 London production was part of the first season of the post-war Old Vic theatre company, funded in part by the relatively new Arts Council of Great Britain and managed by John Burrell, Laurence Olivier and Ralph Richardson. Produced in conjunction with the Joint Council of the National Theatre, the play became embedded in a post-war initiative to construct a proto National Theatre organisation (see Guthrie 1987). Staged at the New Theatre, the production was the last by Priestley to be directed by Basil Dean, and starred Ralph Richardson and Alec Guinness. For Priestley it was a 'star-studded' performance, but the 'stars' did not find it an easy production to work on (Priestley 1977: 79). Richardson and Dean, with the distance of war as an interruption to their professional relationship, no longer found it easy to work with one another, despite the fact that they had worked together on a number of Priestley plays previously (Clough 1989: 203; Dean 1973: 271). Equally, the relationship between Richardson and Guinness became strained (Guinness 1986: 270), but this was not the reason for the production's destiny of relative historical obscurity.

Dean realised that the Moscow production was more aesthetically 'adventurous' than either he or, so he thought, English audiences would be used to but noted that Tairov's had been an 'impressionistic production, which the author regarded more favourably than [his] realistic one'; he felt that the 'war-torn' London theatre was not 'in the mood for such presentation' (Dean 1973: 271). Priestley's own stage directions at the beginning of the printed play text – published after the London production – go some way toward suggesting how the set might have looked in the original production: he states that the set, if realistic, 'should be swung back' and the dining table moved during each act (Priestley 1994: 161). Stephen Daldry and his designer Ian MacNeil have suggested that in fact it was the stage manager of the original production who came up with the idea rather than Priestley or Dean.[2] Either way, the production team tried to solve the scenographic challenge of changing the audience's perspective of the dining room, which the Tairov production had managed to raise and solve earlier. Dean's own description of what he considered the innovative element of the production gives the clearest picture.

> We did, however, introduce one novel idea into the produc-
> tion. The action takes place in the dining room of a middle-
> class house of the industrial Midlands in the year 1912. In
> order to give some variety to the grouping of what was
> basically a static play, the characters, the scenery and furni-
> ture were rearranged after each act, so that the audience saw
> the room from a different angle. Thus an actor who was
> facing the audience at the end of one act might find himself
> turned away from them at the beginning of the next. This was
> Priestley's idea; it proved extraordinarily difficult to work out
> in detail, since the relative positions of all the actors had to
> be adjusted for each act to conform to the audience's different
> viewpoint.
>
> (Dean 1973: 271)

This intriguing scenographic strategy allows for predetermined differentials in terms of visual angles and focus in much the same way as a film might do. The audience's perspective is literally guided by the manipulation of the elements which go together to create the internal aspects of the set: the furniture and some of the flats are moved, to make it seem as if you are seeing the room from a different position. Dean indicates that this was problematic and Priestley's later response in the printed version of the play was that if such a strategy proves too difficult then the director should 'dispense with an ordinary realistic set' altogether (Priestley 1994:161). Priestley recognised in 1946 that the play presented the kind of radical aesthetic challenge which Daldry took up over forty years later. Whether the idea worked in practice or not, it was clearly inspired by Tairov's centralising of the dining table and all that it could be expected to signify in theatrical terms. Reviews also suggest that Kathleen Anker's design with its 'claret-hued' wallpaper,[3] and dark red and mahogany colour scheme, the 'prophetically coloured dark red with the congealed blood of future wars',[4] also mirrored the tone of the Tairov production.

Critical reception

The London production represented the only contemporary drama in the Old Vic season of 1946 and a number of the critics framed it in this context. John Allen welcomed the new production as part of the valuable work that the Old Vic company was undertaking, in terms of the 'inception of big developments in the theatre'.[5] The Old Vic incentive, one of the first to receive government subsidy, was seen as representing the beginnings of an attempt to establish a 'national' theatre removed from the commercial management system, and it was seen as a testimonial to Priestley's achievements that he should be part of this process. Allen, along with a number of other critics and reviewers, made connections between Priestley's *Dangerous Corner* and *An Inspector Calls*, not only because of the thriller/detective element at the centre of the plot, but also because of the portrayal of the comfortable middle class in crisis. For Allen it was ultimately a 'morality . . . raised . . . above the level of the tea-cup drama by the most subtle intensity of writing'.[6] Stephen Potter (writing in the *New Statesman*) gave a similarly positive response, feeling that the 'contemporary moral', contrary to the views of those who had received the production less favourably, had been kept at a distance through the setting of the action in 1912.[7] In contrast Lionel Hale felt that the Edwardian setting was an 'indication of the play's lack of theatrical truth'.[8] This is in line with many of the negative reviews of the production which focused on the politics of the piece and the ways in which Priestley was seen to be proselytising left-wing politics to a theatre audience hungry for entertainment. The reviewer for *The Times* opened his review with the following:

> Bang! Bang! Mr. Priestley lets drive with both barrels. If the purse-proud individualists who overlook their responsibilities to the rest of the human family are not brought down on the plane of realism they can hardly hope to escape him on the plane of fantasy.[9]

Critical reactions to the play, to some extent, reveal the ideological bias of the reviewers, many of whom were aligned more to the political right than left. For James Agate, the play lacked action: everything that 'happens takes place before the play begins', it was 'a modern morality in which nobody does anything except talk'.[10] J.C. Trewin noted what he saw as Priestley's sermonising, and that there was a lack of clarity as to what the inspector was supposed to represent: 'He may be an embodiment of Conscience or the representative of a celestial Watch Committee' – either way he felt that the play, even though short, could have been halved in length and that Priestley's portrayal of the Birlings represented a 'prolonged clatter of skeletons'. For Trewin, the play dealt with issues that were no longer relevant.[11]

There is no other Priestley play for which the initial critical reactions were so clearly split between the political left and the political right. Priestley felt that the original London production had been given a largely unenthusiastic reception in 1946, because the 'selfishness and callousness' which the text explores was less evident or topical in the immediate post-war setting. The British people, still living under the limitations of food and goods rationing, had pulled together as a community during the war (Priestley 1973: 79). Yet the play was warmly received in other countries – for example Russia and Germany – where post-war economics meant that everyday social conditions were worse those in Britain. What Priestley saw as a 'cool, almost hostile reception' (Priestley 1962: 195) by the critics, arguably had far more to do with the shift in the British political scene than it did the audience's acceptance of the ideological stance of the play. The cultural anxiety embedded for the political right in the outcome of the landslide Labour victory of 1945 foregrounded the distinctions between what was considered to be political left and right in public discourse. Although the movement of wartime radicalism, in which Priestley had played a significant role, was 'never really fully exploited' (McKibbin 2000: 534), at the time of the original production, there was a heightened sensitivity towards what was seen as 'leftism'. Stephen Potter summarised the relationship of this sensitivity to the reception of *An Inspector Calls* with the most accuracy.

> It was a shock after enjoying the play at the New Theatre . . . to find that I ought not to have been so pleased with it after all. A friend told me it was all politics, a critic that Ralph Richardson was the mouthpiece of the author, somebody else that it was a pity that for this occasion Mr. Priestley had changed down to low gear and was grinding away again. . . . [S]urely it was the critic, and not Mr. Priestley, who was being politically minded when he dissected the play in the brutal modern manner, by splitting it into Left and Right.[12]

Production III: *The Celluloid Inspector*, 1954

Produced by Priestley's agent A.D. Peters and directed by Guy Hamilton, the 1954 film version of *An Inspector Calls* starred the well-loved character actor Alastair Sim as Inspector Poole (note the change in name).[13] Released by British Lion Films, Hamilton's film created mass circulation for *An Inspector Calls* which had previously been seen only by limited theatre audiences in Britain. Recently digitised, it was successful at the time of release but has also been screened many times since on terrestrial and cable television (Sierz 1999: 239). Despite the change of name to Poole, the celluloid inspector takes on more overtly 'other worldly' characteristics than in the stage version. He does not enter, announced by the maid, through the front door, but rather, through the open French windows while the Birlings are mid-conversation. Similarly, he does not leave through the front door, but merely disappears from the room in which the Birlings have left him: all that remains of his presence is the gentle rocking of the chair in which he has been sitting. Poole consults his pocket watch very deliberately on a number of occasions, as if he is expecting the next event in the plot to take place at a specified time, as if he has already seen the future. His manner, although facially melodramatic – raising his eyebrows and manipulating his facial muscles without subtlety – is physically relaxed. He waits patiently for the family to cooperate while sitting on the chair: he takes command of the space, gently refusing to move or leave when asked.

The film focuses heavily on facial gestures and reactions while at the same time the actors have a very contemporary physicality.

Figure 10 An Inspector Calls, film directed by Guy Hamilton, 1954.

Brian Forbes as Eric Birling and Eileen Moore as Sheila Birling have more in common with young lead actors in a film with a contemporary setting than they do with actors in a period piece: Forbes moves like a young rebel, leading with the head and holding his cigarette between two fingers and thumb and Moore's hairstyle and low-cut, off-the-shoulder dress place them both firmly in the 1950s. The camera shots in the confessional scenes all focus on the upper third of the body, honing in on facial reactions whenever possible.

In this way the characters' emotional responses are spelled out for the audience, as is the story, whereby scenes only described in the play are actually realised in the film. Thus, Eva Smith, who never actually appears in the stage version, is a strong presence in the film, where she is shown working at the factory, and at the milliners, socialising in the variety hall, living in Croft's flat, petitioning Mrs Birling's charitable organisation for money and finally, in a seedy rented room with Eric Birling. Making Smith visible removes her 'every-woman status' so prevalent in the play, at the same time as making more real her ordeal and the family's role in her final destiny. Similarly the visual distinction between the 'haves' and the 'have nots' is given more emphasis in the film. Eva Smith's clothes are simple and plain throughout, while the Birling women dress luxuriously in fitting with their velvet and brocade, high-ceilinged and ornate home setting. The film also stresses class distinctions in setting – the factory floor is juxtaposed with the factory office; the bar of the variety hall with the tasteful modernity of Gerald Croft's bachelor flat; the austerity of the hall in which Mrs Birling's charity holds its 'hearings' with the over-stuffed comfort of the Birlings' dining room. Guy Hamilton draws out the dramaturgical tensions of the play through the visual possibilities of the film medium and in doing so loses some of the subtlety of the text: the audience 'read' the text through the visual rather than visualising through their imaginations, the position of the text in terms of its storytelling potential has shifted – the film was made for a broader spectrum of classes, a popular audience not a theatre one. For Hughes, the film 'gave the public a "good thriller" but dissipated the intensity and removed the peculiar quality of the play', a rather dismissive response, which reveals assumptions about the capacity of film to signify as force-fully as a play text (Hughes 1958: 200).

The dining table, however, remains central, with the opening shots of the film showing us only the table and the food left over from the celebratory meal, rather than the bodies of the people whose conversations we can hear. The Birlings' accents clearly place them among the upper-middle classes of middle England, in contrast to the 'working-class' accents of Eva Smith and her co-workers or the Birlings' maid who speaks only at the end of the film.

Sierz (1999) has suggested that when originally released and through subsequent screenings, the film created a 'cultural penetration' which the stage version had not achieved at the time, and that its naturalistic style meant that one of the key issues around which the play is built, that of class difference, is shown as 'fixed' and as 'natural' (Sierz 1999: 242). To some extent this is true, but the script was not adapted so heavily that the issue of class is removed from the film, nor is a hierarchy of class difference quite as naturalised as Sierz suggests. Rather, the inclusion of Eva Smith as an actual onscreen body and the division of genera-tions in terms of their change in attitudes during and after the inspector's visit, suggest that some sort of moral and cultural shift has taken place. The shame and genuine regret of the younger generation, grouped in close proximity to one another, is clearly pitted against the stubborn refusal of Mr and Mrs Birling to take any responsibility for Smith's tragic end. Croft, the capitalist businessman, stands away from his former fiancé Sheila, and moves towards the older generation in his attempts to remove any sense of real crisis in the class order.

Production IV: Stephen Daldry's *An Inspector Calls* – The National Theatre and beyond, 1992

Genesis, context and history

It is difficult to separate out the National Theatre's 1992 pro-duction of *An Inspector Calls* from either its subsequent history as a West End and touring event or from the relationship between the production and its director Stephen Daldry. The production had an earlier manifestation at the York Theatre Royal, but it was the London production, in a mainstream subsidised theatre with a substantial budget, which brought to fruition the scenographic ideas Daldry wanted to place onto the text. Artistic director of the Gate Theatre in Notting Hill, London, a theatre with a long history of experimental, non-commercial work, from 1989 to 1992, Daldry was seen by Richard Eyre – the then artistic director of the National Theatre – as someone with fresh ideas who was unafraid of 'difficult' texts. Having worked with European plays at the Gate as well as directing many plays in the regions while working for example at the Crucible Theatre in Sheffield, Daldry had a growing reputation as the *wunderkind* of the British theatre at a time when an injection of 'new' talent was much needed. By 1992 Daldry had already been given the job of Artistic Director of the Royal Court but was offered a slot in the National Theatre season during a period of hand-over from the outgoing Artistic Director of the Royal Court, Max Stafford-Clark. The Royal Court was known as the hot-bed of new writing and so the choice of Daldry, with a reputation for reworking marginal or classical texts, was an interesting one. Equally, Eyre was surprised by Daldry's choice of *An Inspector Calls*: a play popular with amateur companies, which had been part of the English school syllabus for some years, not obviously experimental and rather outdated (Eyre 2003: 181; see also Daldry 1993: 7). For Daldry, however, this was an ideal scenario, a play with which he could exploit his talent for '[t]aking the normally small and making it huge' (Lesser 1997: 46), with a ready-made and potentially lucrative audience and a theatre which had given him an artistic carte blanche.

All the interviews and publicity around the production identify Daldry's desire to revamp the play, or at least to reinvest in its potential as a piece of exciting theatre. He saw Priestley as 'a radical playwright who was trying to break the mould and reinvent theatre for moral purposes'.[14] He also had a very strong political impetus for wanting to work with the play: namely that it questions our roles as individuals within any given society. At this point in British history, a whole generation under Margaret Thatcher's Conservative government had been encouraged to believe that 'there is no such thing as society' and that contrary to Priestley's edict in the play, they were not part of a collective society but isolated individuals. Just as Priestley used the setting of 1912 to force the issue of social reconstruction for a post-war audience, so Daldry saw parallels between the mid-1940s and the political choices which were available in early 1990s Britain: the Thatcher years had bought with them the dismantling of much of the radical and socially democratic thinking which had been part of the vision of 1945.

> There is a generation that has no inkling of that romantic vision of creating a better society. They have been told that we live for ourselves and are not responsible for each other. I wanted to do a play that challenges that . . . when political drama seems to lack vision for humanity, it seemed important to hear a powerful voice from 1945 saying they also had a choice between the individual and society. I think Priestley would have been outraged now to see people on the streets.[15]

Daldry wanted to 'reclaim' the text, 'to restore Priestley's original politics' (Sierz 1999: 241), and saw the play as controversial, rather than an outdated period piece lacking theatrical challenges. What he and his team – which included the designer Ian MacNeil and composer Stephen Warbeck – achieved was to create a production which managed to explore issues of social responsibility at the same time as providing visual spectacle and a sophisticated reading of the original Priestley play: the set combined the expressionistic and the spectacular with the ideologically reflective.

The production has an extraordinary history: opening in the Lyttelton at the National Theatre in 1992, it transferred to the Olivier at the National in January 1993 and then into the West End commercial sector at the Aldwych from 1993 to 1995, then in 1995 at the Garrick Theatre and in 2001 to the Playhouse, where it closed in May 2002, although it was still on a national tour of England in 2005.[16] The American premiere of Daldry's production in New York in 1994 not only saw the number of awards given to Daldry and his team increase to nineteen, but also represented an unusual success story for a transfer from a British subsidised theatre to the American commercial market. In fact the production has an unmatched historical significance because of the fact that, despite being a revival of an 'old' play and not a musical, it ran for so long in the West End, on national and international tour and has as a result become a kind of theatrical phenomenon. Matthew Sweet has noted that as 'Priestley's clarion call for the redistribution of wealth', the play was one of the West End's 'least likely long-distance runners'. Similarly he suggested that the production sustained its popularity because, as the political climate changed so the play 'yielded to different political priorities', that Daldry had created a 'call to arms' for a 1990s audience, similar to the way in which Priestley was attuned to the 'utopianism of Clement Attlee's post-war Labour government' and the British audience of 1946.[17] That the original London production did not find an extended audience for the play in 1946 makes the success of Daldry's production even more extra-ordinary: he created a revisionist version of the play which not only changed his own career, but also re-placed Priestley on the theatrical map. The production was visually stunning and innovative, the text was removed from any notion of a realist framework, the musical score functioned as a score works in film – underpinning and at times driving the action on stage. He kept textual alterations to a minimum then shifted the whole theatrical framework for the realisation of it.

Realisation: a political theatrical spectacular

The contextual framework for the production gave Daldry the financial and artistic freedom to explore ideas originally tried out in the York Theatre Royal production in the late 1980s. Daldry's concept for the production owes much to Tairov's in 1945:

> I've got this idea that the play's really all about 1945 not 1912, and I'd like to set it in two different time periods, put

it in this house high up on stilts and set the whole thing in a
big weird filmic landscape.[18]

But Daldry made the idea behind Tairov's costuming of the
inspector in contemporary 1940s clothing – as opposed to the
Edwardian clothing worn by the rest of the cast – more central
to the production concept as a whole. The set, a kind of scaled-
up doll's house on stilts barely large enough to contain the actors,
was marooned among the cobbled stones and rubble of post-Blitz
Britain. Located upstage right, the house with its large dining table
became less important than its temporal and visual setting: the
significance of the table, so prevalent in previous productions, had
shifted, to be replaced by two time settings placed directly inside
one another. From the opening of the production – when a small
boy comes to the front of the stage, acknowledges the audience
and then tries to switch on the 1940s radio placed stage right –
the audience is made aware of the double time setting. The heavy
red velvet and gold brocade curtain, hanging from the crumbling proscenium arch, opens to Bernard Herrmann's score for
Hitchcock's *Vertigo* (1958) and a crowd of actors in tatty 1940s
costumes enters stage left, our vision of them framed by a large
lamp-post, while the facing of the Edwardian house on stilts is
barely lit up, stage right (Sierz 1999: 24). We hear the Birling
family celebrating the engagement of Sheila and Gerald but can
barely see them through the dim lighting and the rain that fills
the 'distinctly surreal' set on stage (Lesser 1997: 16). Inside the
house all is comfort, while outside the adults and children of post-
Blitz England stand watching in the rain. It is Edna, the maid
barely featured in the original text, who is given a more significant,
although silent, role in the Daldry production. When the inspector
enters the stage, she announces his arrival and then 'raises her arm
towards the house, a gesture that seemingly causes the whole
building to crack open down a vertical seam in its front so that
the walls swing back to expose the family seated within' (Lesser
1997: 25). From this point on the Birlings speak from within the
house, from the balcony, the stairs or actually come onto the stage
out of the time-scale of the house itself. The inspector never enters
the house, and when at the beginning of Act III the house explodes

and tilts forward, spilling its contents onto the stage, the actors no longer have the house as a physical separately secure space from which to operate. Even as the house is slowly and almost imperceptibly put back together, the relationship between the 1912 world of the Birlings and the world of the 1940s stage is interlinked and made inseparable. The 'film noir lighting' which creates shadows on stage and places the play firmly in the realms of a 'thriller' dissipates as the production moves forward, but is fully removed when the inspector's final speech is delivered directly to the lit auditorium: in this way the audience's relationship to the two worlds converged on the stage is restated – they are implicated just as the inspector implicates the Birlings. As one academic reviewer has noted, herein lay Daldry's 'major conceptual notion':

> We are luminously enjoined to judge the social anomie of the frequently sentimentalized Edwardian Age. Along with the increasingly intrusive and solemn, non-speaking 1945

Figure 11 *An Inspector Calls*, directed by Stephen Daldry, National Theatre, London, 1992. Photograph: Ivan Kyncl.

chorus of folk, we of the observing present condemn the moral vacuum, the misplaced values and the deplorable lack of human feeling lurking just beneath the rigid mask of propriety.[19]

Timely for the 1990s, the production mixed filmic and theatrical techniques, just as it played on our conceptions of the time period of the play. For Alex Sierz this created a post-modern feel, whereby historical, aesthetic and thematic elements were self-consciously manipulated (Sierz 1999). Daldry created a self-conscious and self-referential reading of the play, using sophisticated mechanical options, such as the house on stilts which explodes and collapses, more often associated with large-scale lavish musical productions. He constructed the framework of the set – the crumbling proscenium facing and old heavy red velvet curtain – as another means of creating a self-conscious referral to a theatre building far removed from the 1970s concrete, bricks and minimalism of the National Theatre. For Sierz this was a direct result of Daldry's desire, above all else, to make the play speak about class in our own time. For a number of reviewers, however, Daldry's production was perceived as an insult to the complexities of the original play.

Critical reception

Despite its subsequent phenomenal success, some of the initial criticism of the production was harsh. Critics felt that Daldry's perception of the play as a 'political parable' had been allowed to override any alternative readings (Eyre 2003: 195). Wendy Lesser points to John Lahr's criticism of Daldry's production in the *New Yorker*: while the original impetus behind the play was to 'sell socialism' Daldry's 'purpose in restaging the play had been to "sell the idea of *himself* to the British public"' (Lesser 1997: 38–9). Many of the production reviews question Daldry's directorial strategy. Sheridan Morley likened the crashing of the house in Act III to Poe's *The Fall of the House of Usher*, despising the fact that Daldry had added some thirty actors to the cast, as 'witnesses' in the form of the onstage silent onlookers. He interpreted the setting as a beach in which the inspector was forced into 'bellowing his enquiries as if through a megaphone across the sands'. For Morley, the impact of the play had been 'defused and diffused by a gimmicky travesty of the original'.[20] In Michael Arditti's view the production evinced 'so little faith in the play' and was in effect a 'Pirandellian exercise in theatrical ambiguity and a sub-Bunuelian social satire'. Here it was felt that the design concept swamped the play, and Arditti even suggested that the National 'cut out the middle man and substitute tours of the set'.[21] Although Kirsty Milne read more complexity into the layers of the production, she too felt that it was 'weighted down by its own portentousness'.[22]

The majority of reviews, however, praised the way in which Daldry had been able to revamp a play seen in derogatory terms by many as an 'old chestnut' or an 'old warhorse of a play': thus Jack Tinkler's response was that this 'is how a musty, dust-laden classic is polished and re-set to blaze like a new gem in the crown of our cultural heritage'.[23] Daldry's 1994 American production received similarly overt praise where the play itself was critiqued as old fashioned and outdated but the production was, as Vincent Canby suggested, an example of how to take a 'modest idea' – being Priestley's suggestion of creating multiple angles from which to view the characters – and 'run with it into outer theatrical space'.[24] The American critics largely perceived the politics of the play as outmoded, they found Priestley 'predictable' and 'sanctimonious' and the play to be 'rooted in old socialist credos and preaching injunctions'.[25] It was the theatricality of the production which impressed, rather than the ways in which Daldry had attempted to find a way of reinvesting in the ideology of the text. But both Eyre and Quentin Crisp noted that whether or not the play acted as a 'covert poultice for liberalism' (Eyre 2003: 257), New York audiences, who applauded the set as the curtain was raised (Crisp 1996: 210), took to the production with 'rapture' (Eyre 2003: 257).

Despite Michael Codron's assertion that the production would not last longer than three months in the West End, it ran and toured for over ten years (Eyre 2003: 226). To have a play with an essentially socialist message, over forty years old, running in the West End and touring successfully all over the world – in Europe, America and Australasia – for such a length of time was unheard of until Daldry's production of *An Inspector Calls*. For Lesser, he solved the play's spatial problems by removing the constraints of the one-room set and playing with interlocking ideas of time and space; but the potential to do so was already in the text – Priestley had already advised getting rid of a realistic setting altogether. As Tom Priestley has noted, it is hard to believe that a 'tired old play could run for two years' let alone over ten (Armistead 1994). The production, led by a director's aesthetic for an age of 'director's theatre', not only changed the pattern of Daldry's own career, but also relocated Priestley in the public imagination. It earned millions at the box office and also created a renewed interest in Priestley as a radical and experimental playwright; for whatever liberties Daldry had taken in terms of his theatrical framing of the play, he barely changed the text at all, merely finding an aesthetic strategy with which to extract and explore the play's original dramaturgical focus and ideological relevance.

8 *Johnson Over Jordan*

The play: an 'adventure in the theatre'

> But now, with *Johnson* . . . it was a complete change of method that interested me. . . . What I wanted to do was to take my characters out of time. . . . You can do it in a dream play . . . because in our dreams we do actually lead a genuine if very confused, four dimensional existence. In dreams not only are we free of the usual limitations of time and space, not only do we return to our past and probably go forward to our future, but the self that apparently experiences these strange adventures is a more essential self, of no particular age.
>
> (Priestley 1939c: 124–5)

Johnson Over Jordan (1939) was one of Priestley's most experimental plays. In writing it he was pushing at the boundaries of theatricality and the seeming limitations of mid-twentieth century commercial staging practices. The play, centred on the journey of an 'Everyman' figure, Robert Johnson, through the moments between his death and some kind of afterlife, is seemingly rather conventional; it is structured around three acts, focused on the process of recapitulation of a central male figure. One recent critic points to the fact that Johnson goes through an 'enactment' of death through 'denial, anger, bargaining despair and acceptance', a process marked by similar emotional markers to those experiencing grief after the death of a loved one

(Friedman 2006: 81). However, from the opening moments Priestley's desire to create what, in the context of London's West End theatre just before the beginning of the Second World War, was a challenging piece of theatre is obvious. For DeVitis and Kalson it represented a 'landmark occasion' in the London theatre, as a 'biographical morality play' (DeVitis and Kalson 1980: 185). For Rebellato, the play was an attempt on Priestley's part to bid for 'writer's supremacy' and yet the writing became lost in a 'welter of competing attractions' (Rebellato 1999: 72). Perhaps as a result of these combined factors, the play 'had a fate as fantastic as its form' (Priestley 1941a: 207).

Act I opens with Benjamin Britten's musical composition; Priestley had made an exciting choice in using this new, young and experimental composer. The music begins 'fiercely and frighteningly and then sinks into funereal melancholy': the score punctuates and creates an aural landscape for the entire play. The first discernible stage space is the hallway of Johnson's home, a liminal space through which the 'real' domestic spaces – dining room, drawing room – are reached but never seen. The play opens just before a funeral service at Johnson's house: the mourners – Jill, Johnson's widow, Mrs Gregg, his mother-in-law, the Under-taker's Man and so on – all pass through the hallway. As this first scene fades so we meet Johnson, 'his face strongly illuminated against a background of darkness . . . like a man in a delirium' (Priestley 1941a: 7).

Johnson, unaware at first that he is actually dead, operates for the majority of the play in a dream-like state. In writing the play Priestley was influenced by the *Tibetan Book of the Dead* and by the notion of *Bardo*: 'an intermediate state that follows soon after death – "a prolonged dream-like state, in what might be called the fourth dimension of space, filled with hallucinatory visions directly resultant from the mental-content of the percipient"' (Priestley 1939c: 121). Thus Johnson imagines himself to be in his office dictating a letter to his secretary: in fact there are four secretaries, 'blank-faced girls all wearing tortoise-shell glasses and dressed alike' (Priestley 1939c: 8). He then finds himself among a hoard of clerks, secretaries and officials who confuse and disorient him as does the 'Voice from the Loud Speaker': the whole movement of the scenes takes him further into a Kafkaesque world of dehumanised bureaucracy.

After a short meeting with his wife Jill, Johnson's further attempts to fill in the forms he has been given for completion are interrupted by two newspaper boys shouting the headlines, 'All abou' the big dee-saster', 'All abou' the burning of London' (Priestley 1939c: 32). He is then confronted with a younger version of his boss Clayton, and taken back in time to re-experience his first meeting with his mother-in-law. The act then ends with Johnson talking to a skull-masked 'Figure' who offers him money and informs him that the sound coming from the brightly illuminated corridor he (and we) can see is dance-band music from a nightclub into which Johnson rushes headlong.

Act II returns us to the hall of Johnson's home on the day following the funeral. Here his wife and his children Freda and Richard are discussing him. The lights fade and then very slowly a nightclub, lit 'with strange crimson and purple lights', appears before us. All the characters he meets here wear grotesque masks, characters such as Porker, Madame Vulture and Gorilla. This is a nightmare scene where Johnson, moving in and out of focus among the dancing nightclub revellers, becomes slowly more inebriated and disoriented. Unaware of their real identity, Johnson mistakenly stabs his own son and tries to sexually assault his daughter. The character of the Figure from Act I returns and tells Johnson that these 'shadows were of your own making', informs him that he is in fact dead and comfortingly invites him to spend some time at the 'Inn at the End of the World' (Priestley 1939c: 76).

The beginning of Act III takes us back to the hallway in Johnson's house where, two days after the funeral, the atmosphere is warmer and 'more cheerful'. As the conversation between family and friends draws to a close, the light fades and we are taken to the 'Inn'. Here Johnson meets his favourite schoolmaster and even the fictional character of Don Quixote, and we hear voices speaking lines of well-known verse before he meets his children and his wife once again. There is a reconciliation and then we hear the voice of a clergyman coming from somewhere in the distance – this takes us mentally back to the funeral ceremony. Finally the unmasked Figure returns, 'tall, hooded and very impressive. . . .

A golden shaft of light from below, illuminates him and throws and immense shadow on the high curtain at the back' (Priestley 1939c: 113): he tells Johnson that the time has come for him to formally depart from this world and although Johnson struggles with this suggestion, he leaves the stage after his final poetic speech.

> I have been a foolish, greedy and ignorant man;
> Yet I have had my time beneath the sun and stars;
> I have known the returning strength and sweetness of the seasons. . . .
> The earth is nobler than the world we have built upon it . . .
> The world still shifting, dark, half evil.
> But what have I done that I should have a better world,
> Even though there is in me something that will not rest
> Until it sees Paradise . . .?
>
> (Priestley 1939c: 115)

Johnson, in bowler hat and raincoat and carrying his briefcase leaves the stage, which has been '*opened up to its maximum size*' and is bathed in a '*growing intense blue light; the high curtains have gone at the back . . . until at last we see the glitter of the stars in space, and against them the curve of the world's rim*'. Johnson exits against a vast night skylight to the sound of the brass section of the orchestra blaring out triumphantly, drums rolling and cymbals clashing. In this way, Priestley's 'ordinary middle class citizen of our time', having gone back in time – to both real and imagined events – and reassessed his seemingly 'small' life, makes a grand but silent exit against a huge background of light (Priestley 1939c: 116–17).

The play asks a great deal of the audience: they are not given the standard drawing room sets of the average 1930s play, but rather, symbolic spaces with drapes and lighting to aid the imagination. Johnson is not an extraordinary man, but an 'Everyman' whose journey through his actual and imagined past helps him to understand a life he was perhaps too weak or timid to change while alive. Priestley draws him in Jungian terms as 'close to the boundary between consciousness and unconsciousness'

(Priestley 1977: 51): the suggestion is that through a more conscious living of our lives we might take more responsibility for our actions and better understand their impact on others (see also Chapter 4) – and this in the original context of a country on the brink of war is a challenging proposal.

Critical reception

> it is a fascinating though seriously flawed work that over-intellectualises an emotionally powerful subject, relies heavily on stage gimmickry, and fails to develop its characters much beyond the two dimensional.
>
> (Friedman 2006: 76)

Critical responses to the play vary enormously with some biographers and critics mentioning it only in terms of its perceived 'failure' on stage. John Braine divides the critical responses into those who dismissed the play because of its expressionistic elements and those who 'recognised instantly its power and grandeur, its enormous range, its masterly use of new techniques' (Braine 1978: 93). Thus, David Hughes believed that the play was spoilt by 'the crying need for an eloquent vein of poetry that would dispense with some of the deaths-head masks and stagey formalities of dialogue which seemed to be . . . a hangover, too obviously smeared with greasepaint, from the expressionists' (Hughes 1958: 155). For Gareth Lloyd Evans the play's optimism and its lack of overt connection to the context of its writing, removed it from the standard expressionistic work so disliked by the critics (Evans 1964: 135).

More recently critics have seen the play as somehow being out of synchronicity with other of Priestley's stage works: that it was an experiment which achieved little. Yet the experimental tone of the play reverberates in a number of his other plays during the late 1930s and early 1940s – plays such as *Music at Night* (1939), *They Came to a City* (1943), *Desert Highway* (1944) and *Ever Since Paradise* (1947). What many of the critics appear to miss, however, is that *Johnson Over Jordan* is among the most 'theatrical' of Priestley's oeuvres. The text is more of a performance score than a play text, with constant references to the means by which both the stage space needs to be transformed and the atmosphere controlled, by Britten's soundscape and the transformation of one lighting state into another. This, it would appear, is what critics like Friedman and Agate might refer to as 'stage gimmickry'. Moreover, contrary to what has been the common critical perception, Priestley was not writing a play 'about death' but rather one about ways of viewing a life, through intercutting funeral scenes, scenes of emotional recapitulation and so on. He was actually exploiting a form of montage, layering one scene over another. Having originally used the funeral service as a stronger framework, he cut this aspect between the original run of the play and the transfer to the Saville: 'the big Johnson scenes were supposed to be happening within the brief limits of a short funeral service', but it seemed to the audience as if the service was 'lasting all evening'. In retrospect Priestley felt that removing this framework had 'ruined the fine effect of cutting appropriate passages of the funeral service onto Johnson's scenes' (Priestley 1939c:123). Such experimentation with space and form – whereby the space in which characters appear on stage is not overtly stated through realist design – were still rare on the West End stages of the late 1930s. In this way *Johnson Over Jordan*, rarely revived, has not received the close critical attention it deserves as one of Priestley's most complex, difficult and experimental plays.

KEY PRODUCTIONS

Production I: Basil Dean's *Johnson Over Jordan* – extravagance and failure, 1939

Basil Dean's 1939 production of *Johnson Over Jordan* has been historicised as Priestley's least successful play in performance. Opening at the New Theatre in London's West End in February, the production transferred to the Saville in March where it ran until early May of the same year. One academic has suggested that the play 'failed' because of the close proximity of its production to the beginning of the Second World War (Friedman

2006): certainly its subject matter did not embody the escapism which might have appealed to an audience living in an atmosphere of impending war. Arguably, the reasons for its relative failure in terms of the length of production run have more to do with the economics of West End management than with either the impending war or the theme of the play. After all, there are other Priestley plays which originally ran for fewer performances – *Bees on the Boat Deck* (1936), *People at Sea* (1937), *Goodnight Children* (1942) and *Home is Tomorrow* (1948) to name a few – but of all his plays *Johnson Over Jordan* is well ahead of its time in terms of the challenges it poses to a director and producer.

In an essay printed alongside the first edition of the play text, Priestley pointed to the fact that this was to date his most experimental play and the location for the production was to be London, which for Priestley was home to the 'least experimental' theatre in the world. Although the play is not, contrary to historical myth, Priestley's least successful in terms of length of production run, it was the most expensive production of one of his plays in the 1930s, and more importantly, the play with the most 'curious history' (Priestley 1939c: 133). Once again, he saw the short production run as due in part to the financial constraints and management structures of the West End, where potential profit had to be shown very early on in a production run or the theatre owners would give notice in the hope of following up with a more immediately profitable production (see Chapter 2).

Opening amid great publicity, Dean promoted *Johnson Over Jordan* as 'a modern morality . . . written intentionally, in an extreme mixture of styles, realistic dialogue, poetic prose, with a little blank verse thrown in at the end'. The production was marketed as an attempt to 'break fresh ground' alongside pleas for the theatre-going public to support what was to be an expensive experiment.[1] Designed by Edward Carrick (son of stage designer and theorist Edward Gordon Craig) with a musical score by the then unknown Benjamin Britten, the production made use of masks – designed by Elizabeth Haffenden – ballet dancers and experimental lighting, of which Dean wrote in great detail in his autobiography. The set consisted of hessian canvas curtains hung in wide 'sweeping curves from the grid on special tracks', two cycloramas, one 'painted and hung', the other, in front, made of 'blue silk' and 'made to part in the middle'. Each was to 'be lighted as if the other did not exist': the stage was virtually bare with 'hardly any scenery in the accepted sense, just a significant door or window to indicate locality, and a few pieces of furniture for similar purpose' (Dean 1973: 265–6). Writing in 1973, Dean was eager to point out that a bare 'denuded' stage was uncommon in the West End of the 1930s as were the experiments in lighting, which concentrated on 'reflected light rather than spotlights' to create a luminosity, 'the source of which would remain undiscoverable by the audience' (Dean 1973: 266). Dean had 'twelve special projectors with colour change apparatus controlled by tracker wire' designed for the production. These projectors allowed Dean to 'literally' paint the 'draperies with light in sympathy with the mood of the events which Johnson was experiencing' (Dean 1973: 268).

The embracing of such scenographic imagination, innovation and expense was more usually associated with musicals than experimental drama. As Priestley observed:

> it was obvious from the start that with a large cast of actors, ballet dancers, an unusually good orchestra in the pit, a tremendous costume plot, and very expensive lighting effects, our expenses would be on the musical comedy scale.
>
> (Priestley 1939c: 129)

But the production would not have appealed to the types or numbers of audience that would, in financial terms, justify the expenditure. Priestley noted that in the mid-1930s he could mount a production for under £1000 – around £40,000 in today's money (Priestley 1962: 153–4).[2] By comparison, the costs of *Johnson Over Jordan* were phenomenal, amounting to well over £5000 for the original production and the transfer to the Saville theatre – over £200,000 in today's terms. Even with a large cast headed by Ralph Richardson, for whom the play had been written, it was the initial cost of the production, not the everyday running costs, which were crippling. The fees for Dean, Carrick, Haffenden,

Britten and the innovative choreographer Anthony Tudor took about 20 per cent of costs, while the scenery, properties and electrics made up 40 per cent.[3]

The production was to some extent financially doomed from the start. In order to keep the theatre, virtually all seats had to be sold each night, but Priestley noted that the more expensive stall seats stayed pretty much empty throughout the short run at the New Theatre. Advance bookings were low and although the theatre was relatively full, the 'fashionables', as Priestley calls them, those more likely to buy the more expensive seats, 'were absent'. The cast and orchestra were given notice shortly after the opening, but when news got out that the production was to close only weeks into the run, 'the box office was besieged'. At a cost of nearly £1000, and in an economic climate where 'business in the Theatre was generally terrible', Priestley transferred the play and priced all the seats at the lower rate (Priestley 1939c: 137, 138). Even with the transfer, *Johnson Over Jordan* was taken off after less than another two months. With a cast of twenty-three and huge capital outlay, the production could only ever break even at best.

Basil Dean's production ideas were to some extent a reflection of the complex demands of the text, but they were also a result of the years he had spent working in the film industry where budgets were far beyond those in theatre. The play arguably demanded a filmic vision and technique, with its multiple settings and dream-like qualities and its seamless move from one temporal and geographic setting to another. But Dean was criticised for seizing on the play 'as the chance to deploy to the limit all the resources of the theatre', and although Priestley had wanted to bring into the production 'everything that the Theatre could offer' (Priestley 1939c: 133: 129), he later noted that if he were to mount a production of the play again, he would have it done in a 'simpler fashion' (Priestley 2001c: 18). Aspects of the production which Dean explicitly laid out for the audience, as he might have done in film, could have been implied – one or two ballet dancers could have substituted for a whole crowd, the nightclub scene in Act II could have been suggested rather than played out and so on. The text itself, with its mix of styles and locations, could have been played with in a more imaginative, less literal manner.

Figure 12 Johnson Over Jordan (the nightclub scene), directed by Basil Dean, New Theatre, London, 1939. Photograph: Angus McBean.

Critical reception

Paul Taylor has suggested that the publicity campaign which preceded the production backfired because of the expectations which it set up and this is certainly reflected in the very mixed critical response which both the play and the production received (Priestley 2001c). There was what Priestley described as an 'exceptionally wide difference of opinion among critics and playgoers as to the merits of *Johnson*'. This was in part due to the fact that, hostile to experimentation and more beholden to 'fixed and rigid' ideas of what constituted a good play than 'ordinary, fairly intelligent members of the audience', the critics saw 'even less than the laymen' in the play' (Priestley 1939c: 127). Agate (1946) referred to the outdated nature of what he saw as an aping of German Expressionism:

> In this, the most old-fashioned piece he has yet contrived, our author had gone back to the Expressionism of the nineteen-twenties . . . dead almost before it was alive. You know the kind of thing. A business magnate wants to write a letter, whereupon twenty typists appear joggling twenty imaginary typewriters while twenty-one office boys lick twenty imaginary stamps. . . . The whole of the first act is a wilderness of dusty antics of this sort.
>
> (Agate 1946: 82–3)

Priestley (1939c) felt that Agate's failure to critique the complexities of the play was 'lamentable' and just another sign of the unwillingness of theatre critics to encourage and promote experimentation. John Braine has also pointed to the fact that Agate's critical framework showed little understanding of the fact that Expressionism provided abstraction rather than individuation in the way that Priestley had written Robert Johnson as a character (Braine 1978: 93). That Johnson is an 'Everyman', a 'typical specimen of our contemporary kind' (Priestley 1939c: 123) may have appealed to audiences who felt some affinity with his emotional journey back through his own life and forward towards his final reckoning with death, but it did not appeal to less adventurous critics. For them, Johnson seemed 'particularly ill-suited to a journey into spiritual infinity – he whose author had given him no inkling of spiritual understanding in life . . . a man so limited by the standards of this world': as such the play ran 'steeply backwards like an unwinding spring from the lively first act to the sterile, petrified curtain at the last'.[4]

Vincent Brome notes Priestley's comments that friends avoided 'mentioning "this lapse from dramatic sanity"', but that the younger critics found more favour with the production, which had been given the kind of pre-production publicity campaign more in line with those used by the film industry (Brome 1988: 237–8). In reality the division between young and old was not so clear. W.A. Darlington claimed that this was Dean's best theatre production and thought that it was 'certain to have great success', written as it was with 'seriousness of purpose and great dignity of mind': less than a few weeks later he called it a 'spectacular failure'.[5] For Harold Hobson the production had a 'theatrical validity; the writing, acting and production are expert': he urged theatre goers to 'correct hearsay opinion by experience' and go to the Saville to see the transferred production'.[6] Others found it a 'struggling courageous play, an experiment exciting even in its failures'.[7] The critics were split in their appraisal of play and production but it was agreed that while perhaps over-publicised and over-produced, *Johnson Over Jordan* was controversial both as a text and in box office terms.

Production II: Jude Kelly's West Yorkshire Playhouse production – marketing through *Star Trek*, 2001

> not even the presence of Captain Picard could salvage the production from the disaster of 11 September.
>
> (Friedman 2006: 76)

Jude Kelly, then Artistic Director of the West Yorkshire Playhouse in Leeds, instigated a season of plays by J.B. Priestley in 2001. The season included *Dangerous Corner* and *Eden End*,[8] as well as rehearsed readings of other plays such as *Summer Day's Dream*, and was framed by Kelly as an opportunity to introduce

Priestley's work, much of which she considered to be experimental, to a new generation (see Kelly in Priestley 2001c: 8). The season included a new production of *Johnson Over Jordan*, the publicity for which was overwhelmed by the inclusion of Patrick Stewart in the cast. Stewart had been a successful British classical actor, but is internationally better known for his role in the *Star Trek* series in the 1980s, where his character, Captain Jean Luc Picard, became an iconic figure, famed for his courage, intellect, leadership skills and for his commanding presence as the linchpin of the series. Picard brought Stewart international recognition and this was brought to bear on the Kelly production just as Ralph Richardson's celebrity status had on the original production in 1939.

Friedman suggests that the Kelly production somehow failed because of its proximity to the attacks on the World Trade Center in New York on 11 September 2001. In fact the production did not 'fail' at all: it was part of a fixed season of plays in a subsidised theatre, not a West End production. However, just as the publicity

Figure 13 Johnson Over Jordan (Patrick Stewart as Robert Johnson), directed by Jude Kelly, West Yorkshire Playhouse, Leeds, 2001. Photograph: Keith Pattison.

campaign for the original production in 1939, which emphasised the significance of the innovatory and complex staging, could be seen to have somehow been rather overworked, so too the Kelly production was ironically overshadowed by the publicity surrounding the return to the British theatre and especially to Yorkshire, of Patrick Stewart, an 'A list' celebrity performer.

Jude Kelly wanted to re-examine Priestley following on from the success of Daldry's revival of *An Inspector Calls* (see Chapter 6). According to Paul Taylor, who worked on the production as dramaturge, Kelly felt that *Johnson Over Jordan* offered the most 'bracing challenge of any piece in the canon' and it also offered her the opportunity to work with Stewart again. For Taylor the original 'overblown' production values had 'swamped' the significance of Johnson's journey and Kelly wanted to put the significance of Johnson back at the 'centre' of the piece.[9] With a cast of ten, less than half the number of the performers in the original production, and a score for two pianos, Kelly's production relied heavily on Rae Smith's dynamic design, which was much praised by the critics.

> The play opens with Stewart as the solidly respectable clerk Robert Johnson, on his deathbed on the apron stage. His pyjama clad image is web-cammed onto a bare, white wall running the width of the stage behind him which is then kicked down by nightmare figures who emerge to take him on to a Kafkaesque review of his own life.
>
> What is left on the wall is then stripped away entirely to reveal a grotesque nightclub which, in turn, masks a psychiatrists study even further upstage, then, ultimately, dark water suggesting the Jordan of the title. With a bed turning into a grave and . . . the floor opening up as a series of pop-up books, the set reveals endless depths and surprises.[10]

Critical reception

The design embraced technology and the possibility for scenes to merge into one another, just as Daldry had done some nine years earlier. Michael Coveney's review suggests that the design,

Figure 14 *Johnson Over Jordan* (the nightclub scene), directed by
Jude Kelly, West Yorkshire Playhouse, Leeds, 2001.
Photograph: Keith Pattison.

although sophisticated in concept, came across as shoddy and lacking style in production. He felt that the white spongy bricks from the disintegrating wall simply got in the performers' way during the rest of the play and quite bluntly removes all imaginative licence when he complains that Johnson's exit to 'eternity' took place across not a 'sea of rippling waves' as one reviewer suggested,[11] but rather clumsily over a 'sea of black plastic'.[12] A number of reviewers complained of Kelly's updating of the setting and text – the deathbed scene was changed to a hospital bed scene and topical references to homosexual marriage, going 'clubbing' and animal rights campaigns were inserted into the text. With a score for two pianos replacing the original Britten music, many found the aural framing – two ladies playing 'soporific musical doodling'[13] – unsuited to the play or the production. For Coveney, probably the fiercest of the reviewers, the alterations to the play 'remove Priestley's strict contrast between the pre-war sobriety and the effusive. . . . Expressionism of the central episodes. And they misguidedly pander to a modern sensibility'.[14] Equally Rhoda Koenig felt that the production failed to find a link with the essence of the original, that Kelly, in modernising the text, had removed its ability to make just that human connectivity she was seeking in reviving the play in the first place.[15]

For Michael Billington *Johnson Over Jordan* has 'echoes of Kafka and premonitions of Pinter', but these were not borne out in a production, which as with the first one in 1939, was ambitious in terms of staging but more so in terms of framing. Interestingly the critics of Kelly's production all grappled with the text as much as they had done sixty or so years previously. In the early twenty-first century, however, the reception and analysis of the play was embroiled in an overall admiration and desire for reassessment of Priestley's career as well as a recognition that in *Johnson Over Jordan* 'the mundane and the mystical are brought together into particularly affecting relation'.[16] Even so, it would appear that staging what is effectively an Everyman text, albeit one with multiple locations and a large cast, posed similar problems in 2001 as it had done in 1939.

Afterword

The Theatre in England is not solidly planted in the communal mind. It floats uneasily in mid-air, a wobbling
diaphanous thing. Officially it does not exist except for the
purposes of being licensed and taxed, and it is probably
classified with wrestling booths and coconut shies. Children
at school are given Shakespeare to read and often to act, but
when they leave school they soon discover that Shakespeare
and his workshop, the Theatre, do not matter at all. . . .
England has plenty of theatres, but nevertheless it says to the
Theatre: 'I do not see you'. If you retort that I am making
too much fuss about the Theatre, for which you have never
cared, I shall reply that here the Theatre is symbolic of many
different adventures of the spirit, and that England now says
too often: 'I do not see you'.

(*Rain Upon Godshill*: Priestley 1941a: 209)

J.B. Priestley continues to have a number of various and contradictory reputations as a playwright. These are in part born of the
complexity of the ways in which theatre histories and histories of
dramatists' works have been constructed. Priestley largely worked
for the commercial sectors of the industry in his lifetime and these
are the same sectors, perceived as either too commercial or too
populist, which have mostly fallen between the gaps in detailed
academic analyses. During his lifetime, his popularity as a playwright, entwined as it was with his career as a novelist, critic and

journalist, spread far beyond the commercial sectors of the British theatre industry. His work was produced all over continental Europe – for example in Germany, the Netherlands and Russia – and America, by professionals and amateurs alike. Even after his heyday as a playwright from the 1930s to the 1950s, his work continued to be produced on both stage and screen but the landmark revamp of *An Inspector Calls* by Stephen Daldry in 1992 has created a whole new generation for whom Priestley's plays resonate. Apart from *An Inspector Calls* – embedded in the English literature curriculum in England for some time now – plays such as *Dangerous Corner*, *The Linden Tree*, *When We Are Married* and *Time and the Conways* are still the staples of the student and amateur repertoire in both Britain and North America.

Always an industry which falls prey to mirroring itself, the British theatre embraced – albeit with some hesitance at first – the success of the Daldry production, and new productions of Priestley's plays were mounted in the hope of replicating his success. In the publicity for her Priestley season at the West Yorkshire Playhouse in 2001, Jude Kelly consistently referred to her desire to reappraise the playwright, to reinvent his reputation: such a season of his works would have been unlikely without the success of the Daldry production. Both directors saw in Priestley not only a socialist and humanist, but also a playwright who experimented with the relationship between content and form. Both equally recognised the filmic quality of his work. Like Tairov, they saw the ideological specificity of his plays reflected in his desire to push at the aesthetic boundaries of theatre.

> My first intuitive reaction to J.B. Priestley was that he was this old dear with his pipe who had nothing really exciting to say. Then I read his other plays . . . and read about his relationship with Benjamin Britten and with Jung. . . . The explosion of form that he was trying to investigate in these plays feels extraordinarily radical . . . [his] really experimental, challenging work is not part of the theatrical canon . . . [he] was an experimental dramatist in his time.
>
> (Daldry 1993: 6)

The response to Priestley from literary critics is still heavily influenced by the dislike by some of the modernists for his populism, his lack of support for the highbrow and his consequent relegation to the realms of the middle-brow writers of his era. Baxendale reminds us that, even nowadays, Woolf scholars are drawn to her condemnation of him as one of the 'stinking underworld of hack writers' (Baxendale 2007) and points to their ignorant categorisation of Priestley with the political right. Yet much of Priestley's experimentation embraces modernist tendencies: plays such as *Johnson Over Jordan* and *Ever Since Paradise* have more in common with the high modernist aesthetic than they do with the English 'realist tradition'. Literary critics sometimes problematise the diversity of his writing but still herald him as being in a class of his own (Skloot 1970: 431).

There remains a framework for analysis which perpetuates the perceived irreconcilable nature of his popularity, prolific output, politics and the context of much of his theatre work. He continues to be perceived by some as a 'lesser' playwright of the mid-twentieth century, despite the evidence to the contrary. Very few playwrights have experienced a similar level of continual success within such broad social and theatrical contexts. Equally, many other playwrights of the period in which his plays were first produced have been virtually removed from the literary canon, but few have caught the attention of young and artistically ambitious directors in the way in which Priestley has.

Although this volume has barely touched upon plays such as *Desert Highway* (1944), *Dragon's Mouth* (1952) or *The Long Mirror* (1952), or looked at Priestley's film work – some of which can be accessed via the British Film Institute and the British Library – the intention has been to provide a detailed and analytical framework for his ideas about theatre and a range of plays which he wrote for it. Equally, of his many novels I have focused only on those which have theatre and performance at their heart. Others are currently writing books on Priestley's politics and on his literary and political versions of 'England/Englishness' (see Baxendale 2007; Fagge 2008). His son, Tom Priestley, has edited a seminal collection of his writing on theatre (see Priestley 2005) and the relevance of his ideas to many aspects of today's theatre industry is still strongly discernible. His novels and plays are still being reprinted and the J.B. Priestley Society, based in his home town Bradford, England, continues to discuss, publicise and celebrate his work. Rare among his contemporaries, Priestley believed that theatre and literature had a social function. A complex man, and one whose work resists any easy categorisation, he often benefited from the mechanisms of a theatre industry which he despised. But this did not stop him from theorising and campaigning for change: for Priestley, like Brecht, political change and a change in the perceived function and practice of theatre as an art form, is always possible if you show it to be so.

Appendix

London productions and revivals of J.B. Priestley plays 1931–59

Play	Production	Transfer	Number of performances
The Good Companions	His Majesty's 14 May 1931 – 23 Jan 1932	Lyric 25 Jan 1932 – 27 Feb 1932	331
Dangerous Corner	Lyric 17 May 1932 – 24 Sep 1932		150 Prod: Tyrone Guthrie
Laburnum Grove	Duchess 28 Nov 1933 – 11 Aug 1934	Queen's 13 Aug 1934 – 15 Sept 1934	335 Prod: Cedric Hardwicke
Eden End	Duchess 13 Sep 1934 – 2 Feb 1935		162 Prod: Irene Hentschel
Cornelius	Duchess 20 Mar 1935 – 25 May 1935		77 Prod: Basil Dean
Duet in Floodlight	Apollo 4 Jun 1935 – 8 Jun 1935		6
If We All Talked Like the Talkies	Vaudeville 13 Oct 1935		1
Bees on the Boat Deck	Lyric 5 May 1936 – 6 Jun 1936		37

Play	Production	Transfer	Number of performances
Time and the Conways	Duchess 26 Aug 1937 – 12 Mar 1938		225 Prod: Irene Hentschel
I Have Been Here Before	Royalty 22 Sep 1937 – 26 March 1938		210 Prod: Lewis Casson
People at Sea	Apollo 24 Nov 1937 – 1 Jan 1938		43
When We Are Married	St Martin's 11 Oct 1938 – 11 Mar 1939	Princes 27 March 1939 – 24 June 1939	279 Prod: Basil Dean
Dangerous Corner	Westminster 19 Oct 1938 – 17 Dec 1938		69
Johnson Over Jordan	New 22 Feb 1939 – 11 Mar 1939	Saville 21 March 1939 – 6 May 1939	75 Prod: Basil Dean
Music at Night	Westminster 10 Oct 1939 – 16 Dec 1939		79
Cornelius	Westminster 27 Aug 1940 – 7 Sept 1940		15
When We Are Married	Vaudeville 6 Mar 1941 – 15 Mar 1941		12
Goodnight Children	New 5 Feb 1942 – 14 Mar 1942		49
They Came to a City	Globe 21 Apr 1943 – 11 Dec 1943		280 Prod: Irene Hentschel

Play	Production	Transfer	Number of performances
Desert Highway	Playhouse 10 Feb 1944 – 19 Feb 1944 and 7 Mar 1944 – 1 Apr 1944		45 45
How Are They at Home?	Apollo 4 May 1944 – 12 Aug 1944 and 16 Sept 1944 – 14 Oct 1944		164
An Inspector Calls	New 1 Oct 1946 – 14 Mar 1947 (in repertoire)		41 Prod: Basil Dean
I Have Been Here Before	Theatre Royal, Stratford East 26 May 1947 – 7 Jun 1947		16
Ever Since Paradise	New 4 Jun 1947 – 25 Oct 1947		165
The Linden Tree	Duchess 15 Aug 1947 – 21 Aug 1948		422 Dir: Michael Macowan
Eden End	Duchess 26 Aug 1948 – 20 Nov 1948		100
Home is Tomorrow	Cambridge 4 Nov 1948 – 4 Dec 1948		37 Dir: Michael Macowan
The Linden Tree	Theatre Royal, Stratford East 7 Mar 1949 – 12 Mar 1949		8
An Inspector Calls	Theatre Royal, Stratford East 25 Apr 1949 – 30 Apr 1949		8

Play	Production	Transfer	Number of performances
Dangerous Corner	Theatre Royal, Stratford East 29 Aug 1949 – 3 Sep 1949		7
Summer Day's Dream	St Martin's 8 Sep 1949 – 15 Oct 1949		43 Dir: Michael Macowan
The Olympians (Arthur Bliss mus. J.B.P. Libretto)	Covent Garden 29 Sep 1949 – 3 Feb 1950 (In repertoire)		10
Dragon's Mouth with Jacquetta Hawkes	Winter Garden 13 May 1952 – 28 Jun 1952		55
The Long Mirror	Court 29 Oct 1952 – 9 Nov 1952		13
The White Countess	Saville 24 Mar 1954 – 2 7 Mar 1954		5
Mr Kettle and Mrs Moon	Duchess 1 Sep 1955 – 3 Mar 1956		211 Dir: Tony Richardson
The Glass Cage	Piccadilly 26 Apr 1957 – 25 May 1957		35 Crest Theatre Toronto Dir: Henry Kaplan
A Severed Head (adaptation of Iris Murdoch novel)	Opened: Criterion Theatre 27 Jun 1963		Dir: Val May

Notes

1 Life, career and politics

1 Useful archive materials on J.B. Priestley can be found at the Harry Ransom Humanities Research Center, University of Texas, Austin (HRHRC). The archive is made up of donations from the Priestley family (1963 and 1985). The first deposit was collated by Priestley and contains manuscripts and publications as well as a selection of correspondence which he thought would be of interest. The second deposit remains largely uncatalogued. The HRHRC also has the files of A.D. Peters, Priestley's agent. The Theatre Museum (London) and the University of London also have materials on first productions and publications. The University of Bradford Special Collections Archive (Bradford, England) has the most comprehensive holdings of Priestley materials, including a great deal on world productions and original photographs.

2 HRHRC Correspondence file with JBP: n.d.

3 HRHRC Correspondence file with JBP: Storm Jameson, 30 June 1940.

4 HRHRC Correspondence files with JBP: Ernest Bevin, 9 August 1940.

5 HRHRC Correspondence with JBP: Carl Jung, 8 November 1958 and 17 July 1946; see also Schoenl (1998).

6 Interview with Tom Priestley (b. 1932) in March 2006. Priestley's son, Tom Priestley, film and documentary maker, is chairman of the J.B. Priestley Society (Bradford, England) and has edited and annotated many of the republications of his father's work.

7 HRHRC typescript of review of *Oak Leaves and Lavender* (circa 1946).

8 Ibid.

2 The function and practice of theatre

1 Basil Dean, a major director and producer of both theatre and film, later founded ENSA (Entertainments National Service Association) run as an organisation which employed professional actors and theatre workers to provide entertainment for soldiers during the Second World War.

2 *Lost Empires* (2002 [1986]) Goldhill Home Media International (originally Granada Television) www.goldhill.com. DVD no. GH1681-3.

3 The typescript of the unfinished novel is titled *These Our Actors* although the catalogue at the HRHRC lists it as being called *Birmingpool*. The cover sheet includes the following statement by Priestley on the central character in the book: 'I borrowed some of his characteristics from my friend and Theatre colleague Ralph Richardson'. On the typescript itself Priestley noted: 'There are some good things about acting and the Theatre in it, fruits of my own experience'.

4 Tairov was waiting for a translation of *Jenny Villiers* and hoped 'to be able to create, in the result [*sic*] of our common work a really interesting performance, that will for a long time remain on [*sic*] the repertoire of our theatre'. Keen to continue the professional relationship with Priestley, Tairov wanted 'to have the opportunity many a time to show the Russian public the plays of John Priestley' (HRHRC Correspondence file: Tairov to JBP, 17 December 1945). The archive at the University of Bradford Special Collections (UoB) J.B. Priestley Collection contains a great deal on Priestley's work in improving the UK's relationship with the USSR (also see Priestley 1946).

5 HRHRC Correspondence file: James Agate, 6 May 1947.

6 HRHRC A.D. Peters Records files.

7 UoB J.B. Priestley Collection: Accounts file.

8 Ibid.

3 The family, gender and sexual relations

1 See *Illustrated*, 19 April 1941, no. 8 for information on Jane Priestley's work with evacuated and orphaned children at Broxwood Court Hotel in Leominster (copy in UoB J.B. Priestley Collection).

2 *The Times*, 28 April 1932.

3 *New Statesman*, 21 May 1932.

4 *The Times*, 18 May 1932.

5 Lord Chamberlain's Collection, British Library, File 11138, *Dangerous Corner*.

6 *Everyman*, 26 May 1932.

7 *Sunday Times*, 22 May 1932.
8 The play was republished for the first time in 2003 following on from a rehearsed reading during the Priestley season at the West Yorkshire Playhouse in 2001.
9 The original production of *Eden End*, directed by Irene Hentschel, ran at the Duchess theatre in the West End for 162 performances.
10 *Independent*, 19 December 2001.
11 *The Linden Tree* originally ran at the Duchess theatre for 422 performances, a very long run for a West End play in a production context which had changed significantly since the 1939–45 war.
12 *Laburnum Grove* originally ran at the Duchess theatre, and then transferred to the Queen's theatre for a total of 335 performances. Basil Dean later produced a film of the play, directed for Associated Talking Pictures by Carol Reed and starring Edmund Gwenn in 1936.
13 The original production of *Mr Kettle and Mrs Moon* ran for 211 performances and was directed by Tony Richardson, who in 1956 went on to stage John Osborne's *Look Back in Anger*, the play which supposedly shaped a whole new generation of angry young male play; Rebellato 1999).

4 Time and the time plays

1 Dr Maurice Nicoll, a former student of Jung, was one of the key figures responsible for disseminating and deconstructing Ouspensky's ideas for public consumption. His medical status gave credibility to Ouspensky's work during a time when a number of 'pseudo-mystical groups were in operation' in London (Reyner 1981: 50). See also www.eurekaeditions.com.nicoll2.htm.
2 Michael Costell, Introduction to 'The New Age' (a small print journals from the interwar period) in the Modernist Journals project, http:Ildl.lib.brown.edu:8080/exist/mjp.
3 First Night file cuttings: *I Have Been Here Before* (unidentified reviewers), The Theatre Museum, London.

5 Work and visions of dystopia/utopia

1 Holger Klein (2004) 'Home is Utopia: Priestley's vision of an ideal society.' Typescript of the annual lecture of the J.B. Priestley Society, 15 May 2004, University of Bradford (UoB J.B. Priestley Collection).
2 See http://www.jgonline.co.uk/orangetree/whats-on-now-next.asp?ID=146
3 The original London production was directed by Basil Dean and starred Ralph Richardson as Cornelius. It ran for seventy-seven performances and is one of the few plays by Priestley which has not received numerous revivals.

4 The production ran for forty-three performances and the play has rarely been revived, although John Gielgud starred as Dawlish in a BBC adaptation made in the mid-1990s. Gielgud refers to the play as 'little known' and written in 1945. The BBC production was directed by Christopher Morahan, who also directed The Orange Tree revival in 2006 of *The Linden Tree* (Gielgud, in Mangan 2004: 487).

5 Milton Shulman, *Evening Standard*, 9 September 1949, p. 9.

6 Although very favourably received, accumulating good press and discussion in the media all over Britain, the production did not succeed in London. Priestley once more pointed to the inadequacies of the London theatre system, where the production was taken off before audiences could build up in number (see Priestley 1949b).

6 *The Good Companions*

1 A.E. Wilson, 'The Good Companions on the Stage', *The Star*, 15 May 1931.

2 *Theatre World*, June 1931, p. 270.

3 *Punch*, or *The London Charivari*, 27 May 1931, p. 582.

4 Mrs Dangle, 'The Theatre', *Time and Tide*, 23 May 1931.

5 *The Times*, 15 May 1931.

6 Ivor Brown, 'Heart of Oakroyd', *The Week-end Review*, 23 May 1931, p. 779.

7 *The Good Companions*, 1933, reprinted and distributed by Englewood Entertainment, LLC, USA www.englewd.com.

8 See Roger Debris, '1950s British Musical Movies', http://myweb.tiscali.co.uk/britmusical/1950s and 'The Good Companions (1957 film)', http://myweb.tiscali.co.uk/britmusical/tgcessay.htm

9 Ibid.

10 *The Times*, 16 June 2005.

11 *Guardian*, 5 June 1974, p. 9.

12 Letter to Ronald Harwood, UoB J.B. Priestley Collection – *The Good Companions* File, 15 July 1974.

13 *The Good Companions*, sung by the original London cast, 1974, Andor Inc. DRG Records CD 15020.

14 *Guardian*, 5 June 1974.

7 *An Inspector Calls*

1 Noël Coward in a letter to Jack [*sic*] Priestley, 9 January 1947: 'I must write and tell you how immensely I enjoyed it . . . finely written, brilliantly constructed. . . . The end incidentally, was the complete surprise to me that you intended it to be' (HRHRC Correspondence file).

2 See www.aninspectorcalls.com.au/stephendaldry.html

3 Trewin, J.C. (1946) 'Mr. Priestley Calls', *Observer*, Theatre Museum First Night File: October 1946.

4 Stephen Potter, 'An Inspector Calls', *New Statesman*, undated cutting from UoB J.B. Priestley collection: *An Inspector Calls* file.

5 John Allen, 'Inspector at the Vic', undated cutting from UoB J.B. Priestley Collection: *An Inspector Calls* file.

6 Ibid.

7 Stephen Potter, 'An Inspector Calls', *New Statesman*, undated cutting from UoB J.B. Priestley Collection: *An Inspector Calls* file.

8 Lionel Hale, 'Mr. Priestley is up against a dead end', *Daily Mail*, 2 October 1940.

9 *The Times*, 2 October 1946.

10 Undated cutting, Theatre Museum First Night File: October 1946.

11 Trewin, J.C. (1946) 'Mr. Priestley Calls', *Observer*, Theatre Museum First Night File: October 1946.

12 Stephen Potter, 'An Inspector Calls', *New Statesman*, undated cutting from UoB J.B. Priestley Collection: *An Inspector Calls* file.

13 *An Inspector Calls*, 1954 Watergate Productions Ltd. Available as a DVD: Studio Canal: Cinema Club CCD30031.

14 *The Times*, 11 September 1992.

15 Ibid.

16 See www.albemarle-london.com/inspect.html

17 Matthew Sweet, *Independent*, 8 April 2001.

18 See www.aninspectorcalls.com.au/stephendaldry.html

19 Jeffrey S. Miller, 'Review of *An Inspector Calls*', in *Theatre Journal*, 46(3) October 1994, pp. 404–5.

20 *Spectator*, 26 September 1992.

21 *Evening Standard*, 14 September 1992.

22 *Sunday Telegraph*, 9 September 1992.

23 *Daily Mail*, 12 September 1992.

24 *New York Times*, 8 May 1994.

25 *New York Times*, 28 April 1994.

8 *Johnson Over Jordan*

1 *Observer*, 29 January 1939.

2 In 2005 the equivalent value of £500 from 1939 was around £20,650 (see http://eh.net).

3 UoB J.B. Priestley Collection: Theatrical Accounts files for *Johnson Over Jordan*.

4 Anon (1939) 'J.B. Priestley's very material intimations of immortality: *Johnson Over Jordan*', *The Play*, undated cutting, Theatre Museum First Night File.

5 *Daily Telegraph*, 23 February and 4 March 1939.

6 *Observer*, 26 March 1939.
7 *The Times*, 23 February 1939.
8 *Dangerous Corner* was a co-production with London based Really Useful Theatres and transferred into the West End after its run at the West Yorkshire Playhouse in 2001.
9 *Independent*, 12 September 2001.
10 *Express*, 14 September 2001.
11 *Guardian*, 14 September 2001.
12 *Daily Mail*, 14 September 2001.
13 Ibid.
14 Ibid.
15 *Independent*, 14 September 2001.
16 *Independent*, 12 September 2001.

Bibliography

Addison, P. (1977 [1975]) *The Road to 1945*, London: Quartet.

Agate, J. (1945) *A Shorter EGO: Volume one*, London: Harrap.

Agate, J. (1946) *EGO 8: Continuing the autobiography of James Agate*, London: Harrap.

Agate, J. (1947) *A Shorter EGO: Second selection*, London: Readers Union and Harrap.

Agate, J. (1948) *EGO 9: Concluding the autobiography of James Agate*, London: Harrap.

Agate, J. (1949) *A Shorter EGO: Volume three*, London: Harrap.

Armistead, C. (1994) 'Big Winnings from Backing an Old Warhorse', *Guardian*, 10 September.

Atkins, J. (1981) *J.B. Priestley: The last of the sages*, London: John Calder.

Barker, C. (2000) 'The Ghosts of War: Stage ghosts and time slips as a response to war', in C. Barker and M.B. Gale (eds) *British Theatre Between the Wars 1918–1939*, Cambridge: Cambridge University Press.

Barker, C. and Gale, M.B. (eds) (2000) *British Theatre Between the Wars 1918–1939*, Cambridge: Cambridge University Press.

Bason, F. (1931) *Gallery Unreserved*, London: John Heritage.

Baxendale, J. (2001) '"I Had Seen a Lot of Englands": J.B. Priestley, Englishness and the people', *History Workshop Journal*, 51: 87–111.

Baxendale, J. (2007) *Priestley's England*, Manchester: Manchester University Press.

Beaumont, T. (ed.) (1976) *The Selective EGO: The diaries of James Agate*, London: Harrap.

Bell, A.O. (1980) *The Diary of Virginia Woolf Volume 3: 1925–1930*, London: Harcourt Brace.

Billam, G. and Priestley, J.B. (1936) *Spring Tide*, London: Heinemann.

Braine, J. (1978) *J.B. Priestley*, London: Weidenfeld & Nicolson

Branson, N. and Heinemann, M. (1971) *Britain in the Nineteen Thirties*, London: Weidenfeld & Nicolson.

Bratton, J. (2003) *New Readings in Theatre History*, Cambridge: Cambridge University Press.

Brome, V. (1988) *J.B. Priestley*, London: Hamish Hamilton.

Brown, I. (1957) *J.B. Priestley*, London: Longmans, Green.

Carey, J. (1992) *The Intellectuals and the Masses*, London: Faber & Faber.

Chambers, C. (1997) *Peggy: The life of Margaret Ramsay, play agent*, London: Nick Hern.

Chaplin, C. (1936) *Modern Times*, DVD.

Chaplin, C. (1964) *My Autobiography*, London: Bodley Head.

Chothia, J. (1996) *English Drama of the Early Modern Period 1890–1940*, Harlow: Longman.

Clarke, J. and Heinemann, M. (1970) *Culture and Crisis in Britain in the 1930s*, London: Lawrence & Wishart.

Clough, V. (1989) *Sir Ralph Richardson: A life in the theatre*, London: Churchman.

Collins, D. (1994) *Time and the Priestleys: The story of a friendship*, London: Alan Sutton.

Connerton, P. (1989) *How Societies Remember*, Cambridge: Cambridge University Press.

Cook, J. (1997) *Priestley*, London: Bloomsbury.

Cooper, S. (1970) *J.B. Priestley: Portrait of an author*, London: Heinemann.

Cotes, P. (1949) *No Star Nonsense*, London: Theatre Book Club Press.

Cotes, P. (1977) *J.P. – The Man Called Mitch*, London: Paul Elek.

Crisp, Q. (1996) *Resident Alien: The New York diaries*, London: HarperCollins.

Croall, J. (2001) *Gielgud: A theatrical life*, London: Methuen.

Daldry, S. (1993) 'Stephen Daldry Interviewed by Giles Croft', in *Royal National Theatre: Platform Papers 3. Directors*, London: Royal National Theatre Publications.

Davies, A. (1987) *Other Theatres*, London: Macmillan.

Davis, T.C. (2000) *The Economics of the British Stage: 1800–1914*, Cambridge: Cambridge University Press.

Day, A.E. (2001) *J.B. Priestley: An annotated bibliography*, London: Ian Hodgkins.

Dean, B. (1973) *Mind's Eye: An autobiography 1927–1972*, London: Hutchinson.

Deane, P. (ed.) (1998) *History in our Hands: A critical anthology of writings on literature, culture and politics from the 1930s*, London: Leicester University Press.

DeVitis, A.A. and Kalson, A.E. (1980) *J.B. Priestley*, Boston, MA: Twayne.

Dollimore, J. (1998) *Death, Desire and Loss in Western Culture*, London: Penguin.

Drieden, S. (1945) 'Priestley on the Russian Stage', *Theatre World*, October: 25.

Duff, C. (1995) *The Lost Summer: The heyday of the West End theatre*, London: Nick Hern.

Dunbar, J. (1960) *Flora Robson*, London: Harrap.

Dunne, J.W. (1927) *An Experiment with Time*, London: A&C Black.

Dyer, R. (2002 [1992]) *Only Entertainment*, London: Routledge.

Eliot, T.S. (1939) *A Family Reunion: A play*, London: Faber & Faber.

Eliot, T.S. (2001 [1944]) *Four Quartets*, London: Faber & Faber.

Evans, G.L. (1964) *J.B. Priestley: The dramatist*, London: Heinemann.

Eyre, R. (2003) *National Service: Diary of a decade*, London: Bloomsbury.

Fagge, R. (2008) *The Vision of J.B. Priestley*, London: Continuum.

Federation of Theatre Unions (1953) *Theatre Ownership in Britain: A report*, London: Federation of Theatre Unions.

Findlater, R. (1952) *The Unholy Trade*, London: Victor Gollancz.

Friedman, A.W. (2006) 'Death and Beyond in J.B. Priestley's *Johnson Over Jordan*', *New Theatre Quarterly*, 22: 76–90.

Fussell, P. (1975) *The Great War and Modern Memory*, Oxford: Oxford University Press.

Gale, M.B. (1996) *West End Women: Women on the London stage 1918–1962*, London: Routledge.

Gale, M. (2000) 'Errant Nymphs: Women and the inter-war theatre', in C. Barker and M.B. Gale (eds) *British Theatre Between the Wars 1918–1939*, Cambridge: Cambridge University Press.

Gale, M.B. (2004a) 'The London Stage, 1918–1945', in B. Kershaw (ed.) *The Cambridge History of British Theatre, Volume 3 Since 1895*, Cambridge: Cambridge University Press.

Gale, M.B. (2004b) 'Theatre and Drama Between the Wars', in L. Marcus and P. Nicholls (eds) *The Cambridge History of Twentieth Century Literature*, Cambridge: Cambridge University Press.

Gale, M.B. (2005) 'A File on Clemence Dane: Celebrity and marginalisation', in M. Luckhurst and J. Moody (eds) Theatre and Celebrity 1660–2000, London: Palgrave.

Gale, M.B. and Gardner, V. (2004) *Autobiography and Identity: Women, theatre and performance*, Manchester: Manchester University Press.

Gardner, V. (2004) 'Provincial Stages, 1900–1934: Touring and early repertory theatre', in B. Kershaw (ed.) *The Cambridge History of British Theatre, Volume 3 Since 1895*, Cambridge: Cambridge University Press.

Gielgud, J. (1981) *An Actor and his Time*, London: Penguin.

Golovashenko, Y.A. (1970) *Rezhissyorskoe iskusstvo Tairova*, Moscow: Iskusstvo.

Guinness, A. (1986) *Blessings in Disguise*, London: Fontana.

Guinness, A. (1997) *My Name Escapes Me: The diary of a retiring actor*, London: Penguin.

Guthrie, T. (1987 [1960]) *A Life in the Theatre*, London: Columbus.

Halliday, M.A.K. (1982) 'The De-Automization of Grammar: From Priestley's *An Inspector Calls*', in J. Anderson (ed.) *Language, Form and Linguistic Variation*, Amsterdam: John Benjamins.

Hart-Davis, R. (1991) *The Power of Chance*, London: Sinclair-Stevenson.

Harvey, D. (1990) *The Condition of Postmodernity*, Oxford: Blackwell.

Hawkes, J.J. and Priestley, J.B. (1952) *Dragon's Mouth: A dramatic quartet in two parts*, London: Heinemann.

Huggett, R. (1989) *Binkie Beaumont: Eminence grise of the West End theatre 1933–1973*, London: Hodder & Stoughton.

Hughes, D. (1958) *J.B. Priestley: An informal study of his work*, London: Rupert Hart-Davis.

Huyssen, A. (2001) 'Present Pasts: Media, politics, amnesia', in A. Appadurai (ed.) *Globalization*, Durham, NC: Duke University Press.

Innes, C. (1992) *Modern Drama: 1890–1990*, Cambridge: Cambridge University Press.

Jameson, F. (2004) 'The Politics of Utopia', *New Left Review*, 25: 35–54.

Jongh, N. de (1992) *Not in Front of the Audience*, London: Routledge.

Jongh, N. de (2000) *Politics, Prudery and Perversions: The censorship of the English stage 1901–1968*, London: Methuen.

Jung, C.G. (2002 [1946]) *Essays on Contemporary Events*, London: Routledge.

Jung, C.G. (2006 [1958]) *The Undiscovered Self*, London: Routledge.

Kaplan, J. and Stowell, S. (eds) (2000) *Look Back in Pleasure: Noël Coward reconsidered*, London: Methuen.

Kateb, G. (1972) *Utopia and its Enemies*, New York: Schocken.

Kennedy, D. (1989 [1985]) *Granville Barker and the Dream of Theatre*, Cambridge: Cambridge University Press.

Keown, E. (1955) *Peggy Ashcroft*, London: Rockliff.

Kershaw, B. (ed.) (2004) *The Cambridge History of British Theatre Volume 3 Since 1895*, Cambridge: Cambridge University Press.

Klein, H. (1988) *J.B. Priestley's Plays*, London: Macmillan.

Knoblock, E. (1939) *Round the Room*, London: Chapman & Hall.

Konckle, L. (1996) 'J.B. Priestley (1894–1984)', in W. Damastes and K. Kelly (eds) *British Playwrights 1880–1956*, Westport, CT: Greenwood.

Lesser, W. (1997) *A Director Calls: Stephen Daldry and the theatre*, London: Faber & Faber.

Levenson, M. (2004) 'The Time-mind of the Twenties', in L. Marcus and P. Nicholls (eds) *The Cambridge History of Twentieth Century Literature*, Cambridge: Cambridge University Press.

Lewis, J. (1984) *Women in England 1870–1950*, London: Wheatsheaf.

Light, A. (1991) *Forever England: Femininity, literature and conservatism between the wars*, London: Routledge.

Luckhurst, M. (2006) *Dramaturgy: A revolution in the theatre*, Cambridge: Cambridge University Press.

Luckhurst, M. and Moody, J. (eds) (2005) *Theatre and Celebrity in Britain, 1660–2000*, London: Palgrave.

McKibbin, R. (2000 [1998]) *Classes and Cultures: England 1918–1951*, Oxford: Oxford University Press.

Macqueen-Pope, W. (1959) *The Footlights Flickered*, London: Herbert Jenkins.

MacRae, D.G. (ed.) (1967) *The World of J.B. Priestley*, London: Heinemann.

Mander, R. and Mitchenson, J. (1961) *The Theatres of London*, London: Rupert Hart-Davis.

Mangan, R. (ed.) (2004) *Gielgud's Letters*, London: Weidenfeld & Nicolson.

Marshall, N. (1948) *The Other Theatre*, London: John Lehmann.

Miller, J. (1995) *Ralph Richardson: The authorised biography*, London: Sidgwick & Jackson.

Morley, S. (1979) *Gladys Cooper: A biography*, London: Book Club Associates.

Mowat, C. (1955) *Britain Between the Wars*, London: Methuen.

Nicholas, S. (1995) '"Sly Demagogues" and Wartime Radio: J.B. Priestley and the BBC', *Twentieth Century British History*, 6(3): 247–66.

Nicholson, S. (2003) *The Censorship of British Drama 1900–1968, Volume 1: 1900–1932*, Exeter: Exeter University.

Nicholson, S. (2005) *The Censorship of British Drama 1900–1968, Volume II: 1933–1952*, Exeter: Exeter University

Nown, G. (1986) *When the World Was Young: A companion volume to the Granada TV serial, Lost Empires*, London: Ward Lock.

O'Casey, S. (1946) *Oak Leaves and Lavender: Or, a world on wall-paper*, London: Macmillan.

O'Connor, G. (1988) *The Secret Woman: A life of Peggy Ashcroft*, London: Orion.

O'Connor, G. (1999) *Ralph Richardson: An actor's life*, London: Methuen.

O'Connor, G. (2003) *Alec Guinness the Known: A life*, London: Pan.

Osborne, J. (1956) *Look Back in Anger*, Faber & Faber.

Parsons, D. (2004) 'Trauma and War Memory', in L. Marcus and P. Nicholls (eds) *The Cambridge History of Twentieth Century Literature*, Cambridge: Cambridge University Press.

Pellizzi, C. (1935) *The English Drama: The last great phrase*, London: Macmillan.

Platt, L. (2004) *Musical Comedy on the West End Stage, 1890–1939*, London: Palgrave.

Plowright, J. (2001) *And That's Not All: The memoirs of Joan Plowright*, London: Orion.

Pogson, R. (1947) *J.B. Priestley and the Theatre*, Somerset: Triangle Press.

Postlewait, T. (2000) 'Theatre Autobiographies: Some preliminary concerns for the historian', *Assaph: Studies in the Theatre*, 16: 157–72.

Priestley, J.B. (1929) *The Good Companions*, London: Heinemann.

Priestley, J.B. (1934) *English Journey*, London: Heinemann.

Priestley, J.B. (1936a) *Bees on the Boat Deck: A farcical tragedy in two acts*, London: Heinemann.

Priestley, J.B. (1936b) *Cornelius*, London: Samuel French.

Priestley, J.B. (c.1939a) *Birmanpool/These Our Actors*, manuscript of unfinished novel, HRHRC: J.B. Priestley Collection.

Priestley, J.B. (1939b) *I Have Been Here Before*, London: Samuel French.

Priestley, J.B. (1939c) *Johnson Over Jordan*, London: Heinemann.

Priestley, J.B. (1940 [1937]) *Midnight on the Desert*, London: Heinemann.

Priestley, J.B. (1941a [1939]) *Rain Upon Godshill*, London: Heinemann.

Priestley, J.B. (1941b) *Out of the People*, London: Collins.

Priestley, J.B. (1941c) 'The Work of E.N.S.A', *Picture Post*, 28 June: 26–8.

Priestley, J.B. (1944) *Four Plays: Music at Night, The Long Mirror, They Came to a City and Desert Highway*, London: Harper and Brothers.

Priestley, J.B. (1945a [1944]) *How Are They at Home? A topical comedy in two acts*, London: Samuel French.

Priestley, J.B. (1945b) *Letter to a Returning Serviceman*, London: Home & Van Thal.

Priestley, J.B. (1946) *Russian Journey*, London: Writers Group of the Society for Cultural Relations with the USSR.

Priestley, J.B. (1947a) *Jenny Villiers: A story of the theatre*, London: Heinemann.

Priestley, J.B. (1947b) *Theatre Outlook*, London: Nicholson & Watson.

Priestley, J.B. (1947c) *The Arts under Socialism*, London: Turnstile Press.

Priestley, J.B. (1947d) *Three Plays: Dangerous Corner, Time and the Conways and I Have Been Here Before*, London: Pan.

Priestley, J.B. (1949a) *The Plays of J.B. Priestley Volume II*, London: Heinemann.

Priestley, J.B. (1949b) *Home Is Tomorrow*, London: Heinemann.

Priestley, J.B. (1951) *The Priestley Companion*, London: Penguin.

Priestley, J.B. (1953) 'Thoughts in the Wilderness: Block thinking', *New Statesman and Nation*, 31 October: 515–16.

Priestley, J.B. (1955) 'J.B. Priestley Looks Forward to TV of Tomorrow', *TV Mirror*, 5(14): 20–1.

Priestley, J.B. (1956) 'Thoughts on Dr Leavis', *New Statesman*, 10 November.

Priestley, J.B. (1957) *Thoughts in the Wilderness*, London: Heinemann.

Priestley, J.B. (1960) *Literature and Western Man*, New York: Harper and Brothers.

Priestley, J.B. (1962) *Margin Released: A writer's reminiscences and reflections*, London: Heinemann.

Priestley, J.B. (1964) *Man and Time*, London: Aldus.

Priestley, J.B. (1966 [1965]) *Lost Empires*, London: Reprint Society/ Heinemann.

Priestley, J.B. (1967a) *All England Listened: The wartime broadcasts of J.B. Priestley*, New York: Chilmark Press.

Priestley, J.B. (1967b [1923]) *I For One*, New York: Books for Libraries Press.

Priestley, J.B. (1969a) *Essays of Five Decades*, London: Heinemann.

Priestley, J.B. (1969b [1929]) *The Good Companions*, London: Penguin.

Priestley, J.B. (1969c) *The Wonderful World of Theatre*, London: Aldus.

Priestley, J.B. (1970) *The Edwardians*, London: Sphere.

Priestley, J.B. (1972) *Over the Long High Wall: Some reflections and speculations on life, death and time*, London: Heinemann.

Priestley, J.B. (1973 [1957]) *The Art of the Dramatist*, London: Heinemann Educational.

Priestley, J.B. (1974) *Victoria's Heyday*, London: Penguin.

Priestley, J.B. (1975) *Particular Pleasures*, New York: Stein & Day.

Priestley, J.B. (1976) *English Humour*, New York: Stein & Day.

Priestley, J.B. (1977) *Instead of the Trees: A final chapter of auto-biography*, London: Heinemann.

Priestley, J.B. (1984) *The Image Men*, London: Allison & Busby.

Priestley, J.B. (1994) *Time and the Conways and Other Plays: I Have Been Here Before, An Inspector Calls and The Linden Tree*, London: Penguin.

Priestley, J.B. (2001a) *Dangerous Corner*, London: Oberon.

Priestley, J.B. (2001b) *Eden End*, London: Oberon.

Priestley, J.B. (2001c) *Johnson Over Jordan*, London: Oberon.

Priestley, J.B. (2003a) *Plays One: Laburnum Grove, When We Are Married, Mr Kettle and Mrs Moon*, London: Oberon.

Priestley, J.B. (2003b) *Plays Two: They Came to a City, Summer Day's Dream and The Glass Cage*, London: Oberon.

Priestley, J.B. (2005) *The Art of the Dramatist: And other writings on theatre*, selected, edited and introduced by T. Priestley, London: Oberon.

Priestley, J.B. and Knoblock, E. (1928) *Apes and Angels*, London: Methuen.

Priestley, J.B. and Knoblock, E. (1935) *The Good Companions*, London: Samuel French.

Priestley, T. (1997) 'J.B. Priestley and the Campaign for Nuclear Disarmament', in C. Rank (ed.) *City of Peace: Bradford's story*, Bradford: MCB University Press.

Rebellato, D. (1999) *1956 and All That: The making of modern British drama*, London: Routledge.

Reyner, J.H. (1981) *Ouspensky: The unsung genius*, London: Allen & Unwin.

Richards, H. (1931) 'The Lure of the Long Run', *Theatre World*, May: 231.

Roberts, P. (1999) *The Royal Court Theatre and the Modern Stage*, Cambridge: Cambridge University Press.

Rogers, I. (1968) 'The Time Plays of J.B. Priestley', *Extrapolation*, 10: 9–16.

Rose, N. (1985) *The Psychological Complex: Psychology, politics and society in England 1869–1939*, London: Routledge & Kegan Paul.

Rowell, G. and Jackson, A. (1984) *The Repertory Movement: A history of regional theatre in Britain*, Cambridge: Cambridge University Press.

Sandison, G. (1953) *Theatre Ownership in Britain*, London: Federation of Theatre Unions.

Savran, D. (2004) 'Toward a Historiography of the Popular', *Theatre Survey*, 45(2): 211–17.

Schoenl, W. (1998) *C.G. Jung: His friendships with Mary Mellon and J.B. Priestley*, Wilmette, IL: Chiron.

Shepherd, S. and Womack, P. (1996) *English Drama: A cultural history*, Oxford: Blackwell.

Short, E. (1951) *Sixty Years of Theatre*, London: Eyre & Spottiswoode.

Sidnell, M. (1984) *Dances of Death: The group theatre of London in the thirties*, London: Faber & Faber.

Sierz, A. (1999) 'A Postmodernist Calls: Class, conscience and the British theatre', in J. Stokes and A. Reading (eds) *The Media in Britain*, London: Macmillan.

Sinfield, A. (1999) *Out on Stage: Lesbian and gay theatre in the twentieth century*, New Haven, CT: Yale University Press.

Skloot, R. (1970) 'The Time Plays of J.B. Priestley', *Quarterly Journal of Speech*, 56(4): 425–31.

Smith, G. (1957) 'Time Alive: J.W. Dunne and J.B. Priestley', *South Atlantic Quarterly*, 56: 224–33.

Sprigge, E. (1971) *Sybil Thorndike Casson*, London: Victor Gollancz.

Stevens, H. and Howlett, C. (eds) (2000) *Modernist Sexualities*, Manchester: Manchester University Press.

Stokes, J. (1972) *Resistible Theatres: Enterprise and experiment in the late nineteenth century*, London: Paul Elek.

Stokes, J. (1996) '"A Woman of Genius": Rebecca West at the theatre', in M. Booth and J. Kaplan (eds) *The Edwardian Theatre: Essays on performance and the stage*, Cambridge: Cambridge University Press.

Stokes, J. (1999) 'Prodigal and Profligates; Or, a short history of modern British drama', *New Theatre Quarterly*, 15(1): 26–38.

Stokes, J. (2000) 'Body Parts: The success of the thriller in the inter-war years', in C. Barker and M.B. Gale (eds) *British Theatre Between the Wars 1918–1939*, Cambridge: Cambridge University Press.

Taylor, F.W. (1911) *Shop Management*, republished online as www.gutenberg.org/dirs/etext04/shpmg10

Thomson, A. (1986) 'Out of the People: J.B. Priestley as wartime populist', *Journal of the Scottish Labour and History Society*, 21: 4–13.

Thornton, M. (1974) *Jessie Matthews: A biography*, London: Granada.

Trewin, J.C. (1949) *We'll Hear a Play*, London: Carroll & Nicholson.

Trewin, J.C. (1951) *The Theatre Since 1900*, London: Andrew Dakers.

Tynan, K. (1987) *The Life of Kenneth Tynan*, London: Methuen.

Ustinov, P. (1979 [1977]) *Dear Me*, London: Penguin.

Van Druten, J. (1927) 'The Sex Play', *Theatre Arts Monthly*, January: 23–7.

Wansel, J. (1995) *Terence Rattigan: A biography*, London: Fourth Estate.

Waters, C. (1994) 'J.B. Priestley (1894–1984), Englishness and the Politics of Nostalgia', in S. Pedersen and P. Mandler (eds) *After the Victorians: Private conscience and public duty in modern Britain*, London: Routledge.

Wearing, J.P. (1990) *The London Stage: 1930–1939*, Metuchen, NJ: Scarecrow Press.

Wearing, J.P. (1992) *The London Stage: 1940–1949*, Metuchen, NJ: Scarecrow Press.

Wearing, J.P. (1993) *The London Stage: 1950–1959*, Metuchen, NJ: Scarecrow Press.

Weeks, J. (1990) *Coming Out: Homosexual politics in Britain from the nineteenth century to the present*, London: Quartet.

Williams, K. and Matthews, S. (eds) (1997) *Rewriting the Thirties*, London: Longman.

Williams, R. (2005 [1980]) *Culture and Materialism*, London: Verso.

Willis, T. (1991) *Evening All: 50 years over a hot typewriter*, London: Macmillan.

Worrall, N. (1989) *Modernism to Realism on the Soviet Stage*, Cambridge: Cambridge University Press.

Index

Related titles from Routledge

Routledge Modern and Contemporary Dramatists:

Federico García Lorca

'An outstanding and completely contemporary account of Lorca.'
Professor Robert Eaglestone, Royal Holloway,
University of London, UK

'This is a highly innovative study, which will appeal to students and scholars alike.'
Professor David George, University of Wales, UK

Immortalized in death by The Clash, Pablo Neruda, Salvador Dalí, Dmitri Shostakovich and Lindsay Kemp, Federico García Lorca's spectre haunts both contemporary Spain and the cultural landscape beyond.

This study offers a fresh examination of one of the Spanish language's most resonant voices; exploring how the very factors which led to his emergence as a cultural icon also shaped his dramatic output.

The works themselves are also awarded the space that they deserve, combining performance histories with incisive textual analysis to restate Lorca's presence as a playwright of extraordinary vision, in works such as

- *Blood Wedding*
- *The Public*
- *The House of Bernarda Alba*
- *Yerma*

Federico García Lorca is an invaluable new resource for those seeking to understand this complex and multifaceted figure: artist, playwright, director, poet, martyr and in the eyes of many, Spain's 'national dramatist'.

Maria M. Delgado is Professor of Theatre & Screen Arts at Queen Mary, University of London, co-editor of *Contemporary Theatre Review*, and author of *'Other' Spanish Theatres* (2003).

Hbk: 978–0–415–36242–9
Pbk: 978–0–415–36243–6

Available at all good bookshops
For ordering and further information please visit:
www.routledge.com

Related titles from Routledge

Routledge Modern and Contemporary Dramatists:

Susan Glaspell and Sophie Treadwell

Susan Glaspell and Sophie Treadwell presents critical introductions to two of the most significant American dramatists of the early twentieth century. Glaspell and Treadwell led American Theatre from outdated melodrama to the experimentation of great European playwrights like Ibsen, Strindberg and Shaw.

This is the first book to deal with Glaspell and Treadwell's plays from a theatrical, rather than literary, perspective, and presents a comprehensive overview of their work from lesser known plays to seminal productions of *Trifles* and *Machinal*.

Although each woman pursued her own themes, subjects and manner of stage production, this shared volume underscores the theatrical and cultural conditions influencing female playwrights in modern America.

Barbara Ozieblo teaches American Literature at the University of Málaga, Spain. She is the author of *Susan Glaspell: A Critical Biography*, editor of *The Provincetown Players: A Choice of the Shorter Plays* and co-editor of *Disclosing Intertextualities: The Stories, Plays, and Novels of Susan Glaspell*. She is co-founder and President of the Susan Glaspell Society.

Jerry Dickey is Associate Professor of Theatre Arts at the University of Arizona. He is the author of *Sophie Treadwell: a Research and Production Sourcebook* and co-editor of *Broadway's Bravest Woman: Selected Writings of Sophie Treadwell*. His essays on Treadwell have appeared in *A Companion to Twentieth-Century American Drama* and the *Cambridge Companion to American Women Playwrights*.

Hbk: 978–0–415–40485–3
Pbk: 978–0–415–40484–6

Available at all good bookshops
For ordering and further information please visit:
www.routledge.com

Related titles from Routledge

History of European Drama and Theatre

by Erika Fischer-Lichte

This major study reconstructs the vast history of European drama from Greek tragedy through to twentieth-century theatre, focusing on the subject of identity. Throughout history, drama has performed and represented political, religious, national, ethnic, class-related, gendered, and individual concepts of identity. Erika Fischer-Lichte's topics include:

- ancient Greek theatre
- Shakespeare and Elizabethan theatre by Corneille, Racine, Molière
- the Italian commedia dell'arte and its transformations into eighteenth-century drama
- the German Enlightenment – Lessing, Schiller, Goethe, and Lenz
- romanticism by Kleist, Byron, Shelley, Hugo, de Vigny, Musset, Büchner, and Nestroy
- the turn of the century – Ibsen, Strindberg, Chekhov, Stanislavski
- the twentieth century – Craig, Meyerhold, Artaud, O'Neill, Pirandello, Brecht, Beckett, Müller.

Anyone interested in theatre throughout history and today will find this an invaluable source of information.

Hb: 978–0–415–18059–7
Pb: 978–0–415–18060–3

Available at all good bookshops
For ordering and further information please visit:
www.routledge.com